Canadian Chronology

Compiled by

Glen W. Taplin

The Scarecrow Press, Inc.
Metuchen, N.J.   1970

For Bernadine and Marjorie

Foreword

This book started out as an outline for my own use to learn more about our great northern neighbor. I started traveling in Canada in 1939, when a friend and I traveled from our homes in southern Minnesota to visit Winnipeg and the lakes of southern Manitoba. When we crossed the border, the customs official looked at our old Model A Ford, and after learning of our plans, remarked that we would never make it. We did make it. Since that time I have visited all of the provinces and territories and their capitals, most of the national parks and many of the provincial parks. Indeed, for the past several years it seems as though I turn automatically to some hitherto unvisited section of this fascinating country.

When I started on that first trip, I knew nothing of the country except what was shown on the road map. As I continued to visit other places, I started reading about why the cities were where they were, who were the men the monuments were about, why their government was different from ours, the intricacies of the fur trade; all I could find to explain the hundreds of unanswered questions that came to my mind. The more I read, the more interested I became, and the thought occurred to me that other people might be interested in the same things. Thus, the notes I had taken sort of grew into this small book which I hope to share with those who have a similar curiosity.

I have used the chief political figures as the basis for arrangement, not because they were necessarily the most important persons of their times, but because the chronological recital of their terms of office presents a natural continuity. I have tried to use their official titles as they were used at the time the person held the office; in many cases the official title was unobtainable or appeared in different forms, especially in the early days, when the colonial system was in its infancy.

Apparent discrepancies will be noted in the early dates, due to the different calendar systems in use. The French colonists in Canada, being Catholic, followed the direction of Pope Gregory XIII, who in 1582, to introduce his new Gregorian Calendar, decreed that the day after October 4 would be October 15, to bring his calendar into a more exact relation with the sun and the seasons. Elizabethan England, being violently anti-Catholic at the time, continued to use the Julian Calendar in which the year begins March 25 rather than January 1st. Thus, during the period 1582-1752, a French report would have a date ten or eleven days later than the same event or document in the English colonies. An act of Parliament in 1752 ordered that the day after September 2 would be called September 14. The English colonists in Canada, of course, followed the direction of the mother country.

Many of the items in this book were not found in the histories I read; for these I owe my gratitude to the generous assistance of some fine Canadians, a few of whom I would like to mention. Professor W. D. Smith, acting head of the Department of History of the University of Manitoba, and his obliging assistant Mr. R. Matthew Bray; Shirley B. Elliott, Legislative Librarian of the Nova Scotia Legislative Library; Mrs. S. Jensen of the Yukon Department of Travel and Publicity; Inspector W. R. Pilkey, Liason Officer of the Royal Canadian Mounted Police; Mr. S. M. Hodgson, Deputy Commissioner (now Commissioner) of the Government of the Northwest Territories; L. J. Gottselig, Assistant Librarian of the Legislative Library of the Province of Saskatchewan; Mr. K. Matthews of the Memorial University of Newfoundland; Captain Ambrose J. Shea, Private Secretary to His Honor the Lieutenant-Governor of Newfoundland. And my special thanks to my friends at the Oregon State Library, for their cheerful, prompt and courteous attention to my numerous requests for more references.

It is my hope that this small volume will be useful and informative to the student, writer, traveler, teacher or just plain reader who is interested in a concise, factual, objective summary of how Canada came to its present state.

The Chronology is up to date as of November 15, 1968.

Salem, Oregon, 1968   G. W. T.

Table of Contents

Indian Distribution

Main Linguistic Groups

A	Iroquoian		G	Chimmesyan
B	Algonkian		H	Koluschan
C	Athapaskan		I	Skittegetan
D	Salish		J	Siouan
E	Wakashan		K	Beothuk
F	Kutenaian		L	Eskimoan

Main Tribes

1.	Kutchin C	20.	Dog Rib C
2.	Tlingit H	21.	Yellowknife C
3.	Tagish H	22.	Slave C
4.	Kaska C	23.	Sekani C
5.	Tahltan C	24.	Beaver C
6.	Haida I	25.	Sarsi C
7.	Tsetsaut C	26.	Blackfoot B
8.	Tsimshian G	27.	Gros Ventre C
9.	Kwakiutl E	28.	Assiniboine J
10.	Bella Coola D	29.	Copper Eskimo L
11.	Carrier C	30.	Caribou Eskimo L
12.	Chilcotin C	31.	Chipewyan C
13.	Nootka E	32.	Cree B
14.	Coast Salish D	33.	Ojibway B
15.	Interior Salish D	34.	Central Eskimo L
16.	Nicola C	35.	Labrador Eskimo L
17.	Kutenai F	36.	Abnaki B
18.	Mackenzie Eskimo L	37.	Algonkian B
19.	Hare C	38.	Huron (Wyandot) A

Approximate Indian Distribution

European Monarchs Concerned with Canadian History

English

Henry VII. Died April 21, 1509.

Henry VIII. Died January 27, 1547.

Edward VI. Died July 6, 1553.

Mary I. Died November 17, 1558.

Elizabeth I. Died March 24, 1603.

James I. Died March 27, 1625.

Charles I. Beheaded January 30, 1649.

The Commonwealth. Ended December 16, 1653.

Oliver Cromwell, Lord Protector. Died September 3, 1658.

Richard Cromwell, Lord Protector. Abdicated April 22, 1659.

Long Parliament restored. May 7 - October 13, 1659.

Military Government. To December 26, 1659.

Long Parliament restored. To March 16, 1660.

Charles II. Took office May 29, 1660. Died February 6, 1685.

James II. Abdicated December 22, 1688.

William III and Mary II. Took office February 13, 1689.

  Mary died December 28, 1694.

  William died March 8, 1702.

Anne. Died August 1, 1714.

George I. Died June 11, 1727.

George II. Died October 25, 1760.

George III. Died January 29, 1820.

George IV. Died June 26, 1830.

William IV. Died June 20, 1837.

Victoria. Died January 21, 1901.

Edward VII. Died May 6, 1910.

George V. Died January 20, 1936.

Edward VIII. Abdicated December 10, 1936.

George VI. Died February 6, 1952.

Elizabeth II.

<u>French</u>

Charles VIII. Died April 7, 1498.

Louis XII. Died January 1, 1515.

Francis I. Died March 31, 1547.

Henry II. Died July 10, 1559.

Francis II. Died December 5, 1560.

Charles IX. Died May 30, 1574.

Henry III. Died August 2, 1589.

Henry IV. Assassinated May 14, 1610.

Louis XIII. Died May 14, 1643.

Louis XIV. Died September 1, 1715.

Louis XV. Died May 10, 1774.

CANADA - QUEBEC AND ONTARIO

Scandinavian Discovery and Settlement 875-1016

Celt-Irish monks from Iceland, believed to have landed on Brion Island in the Gulf of St. Lawrence, settled on Cape Breton Island, circa 875. Their settlement, called Huitramannaland (Country of the White Men) by Scandinavian writers, was gradually absorbed into the native Micmac population.

Bjarni Herjulfsson. 986. From Iceland, is believed to have sailed along eastern coast from Vinland (Wineland, now Newfoundland) to Markland (Forest Land-now Labrador) to Helluland (Stony Land-now Baffin Island).

Lief Ericson. 1004. From Greenland. Spent winter of 1004-1005 at Vinland (L'Anse au Meadow, Newfoundland).

Thorwald Ericson. 1005-1008. Brother of Lief. Spent two winters in Vinland, was killed there.

Thorfinn Karlsefni. 1012-1016. From Greenland. Married Gudrid, Thorwald's widow. Spent three winters on Vinland, his son Snorre born there, 1013, the first white child to be born in North America. The settlement was abandoned.

Basic Claims 1497-1534

Giovanni Caboto, a Genoese, sailed from Bristol in the Mathew. He landed on Cape Breton Island at Cape St. George, June 24, 1497 and claimed it for his sponsor, King Henry VII of England.

Giovanni de Verrazano, a Florentine, sailed from St. Malo. He explored the Atlantic coast from Spanish Florida to Newfoundland in the summer of 1524 and named the land Francesca in honor of his sponsor, Francis I of France.

15

Jacques Cartier, a Breton navigator sailing from St. Malo, landed at what is now known as Penouille Point, at the entrance of Gaspé, July 24, 1534, and claimed it for Francis I.

He entered the estuary of the St. Lawrence River on August 10, 1535 and reached the Iroquois Indian village of Stadacona (Quebec City) on September 16, 1535. He reached the Huron Indian village of Hochelaga (Montreal) on October 2, 1535 and after wintering at Stadacona, departed for France on May 3, 1536. Cartier died September 1, 1557 at Limoilou near St. Malo.

French Attempt to Settle Canada, 1541-1605

Jean François de la Rocque, Seigneur de Roberval was named Lieutenant-General of the new territory by Francis I, on January 15, 1541, and was granted seigneurial ownership. He retained Cartier as captain-general and master pilot to establish a settlement. Cartier wintered at Cap Rouge, near Stadacona, beginning in August, 1541 and named his settlement Charlesbourg-Royal. When he started the return to France, he met Roberval at St. John's, Newfoundland, June 8, 1542, and on June 18, 1542, continued his return journey. Roberval reached Cartier's settlement in July, 1542, and renamed it France-Royal. He wintered there and then returned to France in September, 1543, taking his colony with him.

Troilus de Mesquoat, Marquis de la Roche, was named Viceroy of New France by Henry III on January 3, 1578. He received a patent to colonize the region and a monopoly of trade, provided that he occupy the territory and found a colony.

On February 16, 1597, he received a grant from Henry IV, empowering him to send an expedition overseas, and on January 12, 1598 was appointed Lieutenant-General of Canada, Newfoundland and Labrador, and given ownership and monopoly of trade. He landed colonists on Sable Island and returned to France in 1598; the colonists were brought home in 1603.

François du Pont-Gravé, merchant of St. Malo, and Pierre

Chauvin, Sieur de Tonnetuit, sea captain, were granted a ten-year monopoly of the fur trade, on November 22, 1599, provided that they settled colonists. When la Roche protested, Chauvin was made his lieutenant and was given exclusive trading privileges along the St. Lawrence River while la Roche was given the trade in Newfoundland, the Gulf of St. Lawrence and the Atlantic Ocean. Chauvin attempted a settlement at Tadoussac in the winter of 1600-1601 but the attempt failed. Chauvin died February, 1603.

Commander Aymar de Chastes was named Lieutenant-General in New France by Henry IV in February, 1602. He obtained a patent for planting colonies and a trading monopoly and formed a trading company under Du Pont-Gravé. Du Pont-Gravé, accompanied by Samuel Champlain, traded as far as Hochelaga during the summer of 1603. De Chastes died May 13, 1603.

Pierre de Guast, Sieur de Monts was named Lieutenant-general in Acadie by Henry IV, on November 8, 1603. He was granted a 10-year monopoly of trade provided that he settle colonists. In 1604, accompanied by Champlain and the Sieur de Poutrincourt he visited Acadie, granted the Port Royal site to Poutrincourt and made a settlement on St. Croix Island off the coast of Maine. This colony was moved to Port Royal in the summer of 1605 after which de Monts returned to France. (For subsequent developments in Acadie, see that chapter).

De Monts' concession was cancelled in 1607. He obtained a one-year trading concession on January 7, 1608 and was named Lieutenant-General of New France. Champlain, sent to the new world as his lieutenant, founded Quebec on July 3, 1608.

New France Under the Trading Companies 1607-1629

Louis de Bourbon, Comte de Soissons was named Governor and Lieutenant-General of New France by his nephew, King Louis XIII, on October 8, 1611. He received seigneural rights and the trading monopoly. He made Champlain his deputy and commander at Quebec. Died November 12, 1611.

Henry de Bourbon, Prince de Condé was named Viceroy of

New France on November 22, 1611, and received the trade monopoly. He retained Champlain as his lieutenant. Champlain organized the trading group known as the Company of Merchants of Rouen and St. Malo, 1614, who paid Condé for the trading concession and agreed to make settlements.

When Condé was arrested on September 1, 1616, and put in the Bastille, De Thémines took over as Lieutenant-General of New France until Condé was released and resumed his office as Viceroy in October, 1619.

Henri, Duc de Montmorency, Admiral of France, bought out the Prince de Condé, and on February 25, 1620, was appointed Viceroy of New France. Champlain was retained as his lieutenant in Quebec. Montmorency cancelled the concession of the Company of Merchants and replaced it with the Company of Montmorency, which was formed by Guillaume de Caen and his nephew Emery on November 8, 1620.

On February 4, 1623, feudalism began in New France, when Montmorency granted the fief of Sault-au-Matelot to Louis Hébert.

Henri de Levis, Duc de Ventadour was named Viceroy in March, 1625, after he bought out Montmorency, his uncle. He continued Champlain as his lieutenant in Quebec.

Armand Jean du Plessis, Cardinal Richelieu, formed the Company of New France, or the One Hundred Associates, on April 29, 1627, and revoked the de Caen charter. An agreement was ratified on May 6, 1628, which gave the Company full seigneurial ownership, a perpetual fur monopoly and a 15-year trade monopoly in Canada, Acadie and Newfoundland. The government was delegated to a Governor nominated by the Company and appointed by the King. The Company was to bring in settlers.

Quebec was taken by the English under Admiral David Kirke, August 9, 1629, and was controlled by a garrison under Lewis Kirke. The conquest was nullified by the Treaty of Susa, April 24, 1629 and the city was restored to the French by the Treaty of St. Germaine-en-Laye, March 29, 1632. The French re-occupied Quebec July 13, 1632.

Governors Under the One Hundred Associates 1633-1663

Samuel Champlain was appointed Lieutenant-General, March 1, 1633, by Richelieu. He died in office, December 25, 1635.

In 1634, Jean Nicolet explored Lake Michigan, and in the same year Trois Rivières was founded by La Biolette. It became the fur-trading center of the colony.

Marc Antoine Brad-de-fer de Chateaufort's terms as Administrator, extended from December 25, 1635 to June 11, 1636.

Charles Jacques Herault de Montmagny was appointed January 15, 1636, and was the first to bear the title of Governor. His term extended from June 11, 1636 to August 19, 1648.

On May 18, 1642, the Ville Marie de Montreal was founded by Paul de Chomeday, Sieur de Maisonneuve, who served as Governor of Ville Marie (Montreal) until removed by the Marquis de Tracy in 1665.

Cardinal Richelieu died on December 4, 1642, and was succeeded by Giulio Cardinal Mazarin as chief minister of France. Louis XIII died on May 14, 1643 and was succeeded by Louis XIV, who was then four years eight months old.

Iroquois hostilities against the French began on August 3, 1643, with the capture and torture of Father Isaac Joques at Lac St. Pierre.

On March 6, 1645, the King's Council, by Order-in-Council, ratified an agreement whereby the One Hundred Associates would sublet the fur trading monopoly, to residents of the colony, retaining for themselves the seigneurial ownership, excluding Acadie. The colonial company organized under the name Compagnie des Habitants.

In further reorganization, on March 27, 1647, Louis XIV issued an edict setting up the Council of Quebec. The Council was to be composed of the Governor of Quebec, the Superior of the Jesuits until a bishop should arrive, and the Governor of Montreal; it was to govern the country on behalf of the One Hundred Associates. The Council was to govern in all matters of finance, fur trade and general policy; representatives from Quebec, Montreal and Trois Riviérs were entitled to attend meetings and express sentiments.

Louis d'Ailleboust, Sieur de Coulonge was appointed Governor on March 2, 1648. His term extended from August 20, 1648 to October 12, 1651.

Jean de Lauzon was appointed Governor on January 17, 1651; his term extended from October 14, 1651 to September 12, 1657. He left on September, 1656, leaving his son Charles de Lauzon-Charney as Administrator.

Louis d'Ailleboust, Sieur de Coulonge was administrator from September 13, 1657 to July 11, 1658.

Pierre de Voyer, Vicomte d'Argenson was appointed Governor on January 26, 1657. His term extended from July 11, 1658 to August 31, 1661.

In 1659 Pierre Esprit Radisson and Médard Chouart des Groseilliers got to the upper Mississippi country and they reached to James Bay, 1661.

François de Montmorency, Monseigneur de Laval was appointed Bishop of Petrea and Vicar-apostolic in New France, on June 8, 1658. He arrived in Quebec June 16, 1659, as acting Bishop of Quebec.

Pierre de Bois, Baron d'Avaugour was Governor from August 31, 1661 to July 23, 1663.

Cardinal Mazarin died March 9, 1661 and Jean Baptiste Colbert became chief minister of France.

On February 24, 1663, the One Hundred Associates executed a deed conveying to the Crown all their interests in Canada, making New France a Royal Colony. In an edict of March 21, 1663, Louis XIV revoked all grants made by the Company of lands which had not been cleared six months after the date of the grant.

An edict of Louis XIV in May 1664, established La Compaigne des Indies Occidentales to carry on trading functions in New France. This company was discontinued ten years later by the edict of December, 1674.

The Old Regime 1663-1760

By the Edit de Création du Conseil Souverain, April, 1663,

authority in New France was vested in a Sovereign Council; the name was changed in 1703 to the Superior Council. The Governor was the political and military head, the King's representative in the colony. The Bishop of Quebec was the spiritual head and the Intendant was the head of administration. Advice was furnished by five councillors selected by the Governor and the Bishop.

Charles Augustine de Saffray, Sieur de Mezy, was appointed Governor on May 1, 1663. His term extended from August 15, 1663 to May 5, 1665, when he died in office.

Sieur Louis Robert was appointed Intendant on March 21, 1663, but never came to New France, and the appointment was cancelled May 7, 1663.

Monseigneur Laval continued as acting Bishop of Quebec.

Alexandre de Prouville, Marquis de Tracy, Lieutenant-General of the French dominions in the New World (1663-1667), arrived with the Carignan-Salière Regiment on June 30, 1665, to remove the Mohawk Iroquois menace.

Jacques le Neuf de la Potheric was Administrator from May 6, 1665 to September 12, 1665.

Daniel de Rémy, Sieur de Courcelle was appointed Governor on March 23, 1665. His term ran from September 12, 1665 to September 12, 1672.

Jean Talon was appointed Intendant on March 23, 1665 and his term extended from September 23, 1665 to October 22, 1668.

Claude de Couteroue was appointed Intendant on April 8, 1668; he served from October 22, 1668 to October 22, 1670.

Jean Talon was reappointed as Intendant on May 14, 1669; his term ran from October 23, 1670 to October, 1672.

Monseigneur Laval was officially appointed Bishop of Quebec on October 1, 1674.

René Cavalier, Sieur de la Salle, reached the Ohio River, 1669-1670 and the Illinois River 1670-1671. Simon François Daumont, Sieur de Saint-Lusson and Father Allouez, Jesuit, claimed the area around Lake Superior, at Sault Ste. Marie, June 14, 1671. Paul Denis de Saint-Simon and Father Albanel claimed the area around James Bay, on June 28, 1672, at Fort Charles on the Rupert River.

Louis de Buade, Comte de Frontenac, was Governor from September 12, 1672 to May 9, 1682.

Frontenac acted as Intendant from September 12, 1672 to September 16, 1675.

Jacques Duchesneau was appointed Intendant on May 30, 1675; term extended from September 16, 1675 to May 9, 1682.

Bishop Laval continued in office.

Louis Joliet and Father Jacques Marquette discovered the Mississippi River on June 17, 1672.

LaSalle reached the mouth of the Mississippi, and claimed the land for France on April 9, 1682.

Joseph Le Febvre, Sieur de la Barre was appointed Governor on May 1, 1682; he served from October 9, 1682 to March 10, 1685.

Jacques de Meulles was appointed Intendant on May 1, 1682; he served from October 9, 1682 to September 23, 1686.

Bishop Laval continued in office.

Jacques René de Brisey, Marquis de Denonville was appointed Governor on January 1, 1685; his term extended from August 1, 1685 to August 12, 1689.

Jean Buchart, Chevalier de Champigny was appointed Intendant on April 24, 1686; his term extended from September 23, 1686 to October 5, 1702.

Bishop Laval resigned January 24, 1688; he died May 6, 1708, at Quebec.

Jean Baptiste de la Croix de Chevrières Monseigneur de Saint-Vallier was appointed Bishop on January 25, 1688.

Governor Denonville was recalled for military service in Europe on May 31, 1689, but was still in New France on August 4, 1689 when the Iroquois renewed hostilities by the Lachine massacre.

Louis de Buade, Comte de Frontenac was again appointed Governor. His term extended from August 12, 1689 to November 28, 1698. He died in office.

Buchart continued as Intendant.

Saint-Vallier continued as Bishop.

Louis Hector de Callières was Administrator from November 29, 1698 to September 13, 1699. He was appointed Governor on April 20, 1699; and his term ran from September 14, 1699 to May 26, 1703. He died in office.

François de Beauharnais was appointed Intendant on April 1, 1702; he served from October 5, 1702 to September 17, 1705. Saint-Vallier continued as Bishop.

Detroit was founded by Antoine de LaMothe-Cadillac, on July 24, 1701.

Peace was concluded with the Iroquois confederation at Montreal, on August 4, 1701.

Philippe de Rigaud, Marquis de Vaudreuil-Cavagnal served as Administrator from May 27, 1703 to September 16, 1705. He was appointed Governor on August 1, 1703. He served from September 17, 1705 to October 10, 1725, dying in office.

Jacques Raudot was appointed Intendant on January 1, 1705; he served from September 17, 1705 to November 6, 1711.

Michel Bégon de la Picardière was appointed Intendant on March 31, 1710; his term extended from November 7, 1711 to September 2, 1726.

Edmé Nicolas Robert was appointed Intendant on February 22, 1724, but did not serve.

Guillaume de Chazelles was appointed Intendant in 1725, but died in a shipwreck near Louisbourg, on August 25, 1725, enroute to Quebec. Bégon continued on as interim Intendant. Saint-Valliere continued as Bishop.

Charles LeMoyne, 1st Baron de Longueuil was Administrator from August 11, 1725 to September 2, 1726.

Charles de la Boische, Marquis de Beauharnais was appointed Governor on January 11, 1726. He served from September 2, 1726 to September 19, 1747.

Claude-Thomas Dupuy was appointed Intendant on November 23, 1725; he served from August 28, 1726 to August 30, 1728.

Gilles Hocquart was appointed Intendant on February 21, 1731; he served from August 20, 1731 to September 2, 1748.

Bishop Saint-Vallier died in office on December 26, 1727.

Louis François Duplessis de Mornay was appointed Bishop on December 26, 1727 and resigned on September 12, 1733.

Pierre Herman Dosquet was appointed Bishop on September 12, 1733 and resigned on June 25, 1739.

François Louis Pourroy de Laubervivière was appointed Bishop on June 25, 1739. He died in office on August 20, 1740.

Henri Marie Dubreuil de Pontbriand was appointed Bishop on March 6, 1741. He died in office on June 8, 1760 in Montreal. He was the last Bishop before the English conquest.

Roland Michel Barrin, Comte de la Galissonière, served as Administrator from September 19, 1747 to August 14, 1749.

François Bigot was appointed Intendant on January 7, 1748; he served from September 2, 1748 to September 8, 1760. He was found guilty of malfeasance in office on December 10, 1763, in Paris, and was exiled from France. Bigot died at Neuchatel, Switzerland on January 12, 1778.

Jacques-Pierre de Taffanel, Marquis de la Jonquière was appointed Governor on March 15, 1746, but was captured by the British and did not arrive in Quebec until August 15, 1749. He died in office on May 17, 1752.

Charles LeMoyne, 2nd Baron de Longueuil served as Administrator from May 17, 1752 to July, 1752.

Marquis Duquesne de Menneville was appointed Governor on January 1, 1752. He served from July, 1752 to June 24, 1755.

Duquesne directed the building of fortifications along the Ohio River and lower Lake Huron. Ft. Duquesne, later Pittsburg, founded on April 17, 1754, was named for him.

Pierre de Rigaud, Marquis de Vaudreuil-Cavagnal, son of a former Governor, was appointed Governor on January 1, 1755; he served from July 10, 1755 to September 8, 1760.

New France was divided into three districts with centers at Quebec, Montreal and Trois Rivières.

The French and Indian War in North America, corresponding to the Seven Years War in Europe, started when Great Britain declared war on May 17, 1756 and France declared war on June 16, 1756.

Quebec was defended by Louis Joseph, Marquis de Montcalm, but when it was surrendered to the British, on September 13, 1759, it was under Brevet-Major General James Wolfe. Both commanders were killed and the city was surrendered to the English under General Townshend and Admiral Saunders, by Commander Ramezay.

François Gaston, Duc de Lévis, succeeded Montcalm as Commander-in-Chief of the French forces. Governor Vaudreuil surrendered Montreal to General Jeffrey Amherst, Commander-in Chief of British forces, on September 8, 1760. Colonel Frederick Haldimand took possession for the British, completing the conquest.

British Military Governors, 1760-1763

Canada was under military government until after the Treaty of Paris. The Commander-in-Chief was General Jeffrey Amherst, who resided in New York City. Amherst had been appointed Commander-in-Chief after the capture of Louisbourg, July, 1758, and was appointed Governor-General of British North America after the fall of Montreal in 1760.

Three governments were set up in Canada, each reporting to Amherst. Quebec, formed on September 18, 1759, was governed by Brigadier-General James Murray, who was appointed on October 23, 1759. After the fall of Montreal, Amherst appointed Brigadier-General Thomas Gage to command in Montreal and Colonel Ralph Burton to command in Three Rivers; both were appointed on September 22, 1760.

In October, 1763, General Gage succeeded Amherst as Commander-in-Chief in New York City, and Colonel Burton from Three Rivers took over his command in Montreal. The Three Rivers command was given to Colonel Frederick Haldimand. General Murray remained in Quebec until civil government was established on August 10, 1764. He was appointed Canada's first British Governor.

Governors of Quebec 1763-1791

By the Treaty of Paris, February 10, 1763, France renounced all claims in North America except for the islands of St. Pierre and Miquelon, which she retains to this day.

A Royal Proclamation, on October 7, 1763, set the boundaries and established the government of Quebec. The territory included in the Province of Quebec was, roughly, the valley of the St. Lawrence River from Nova Scotia on the east to Lake Nipissing on the west. Quebec was to be ruled by a Governor appointed by the Crown, who was to legislate with the advice of a council and a general assembly, which he had power to summon. In practice, the assembly was never summoned under the Proclamation of 1763.

Brigadier-General James Murray was appointed Governor on November 21, 1763. His term began on August 13, 1763. He was recalled on April 1, 1766, and left Canada on June 28, 1766, however he remained Governor until April 12, 1768.

Paulus A. Irving, President of the Council, acted as Administrator from June 30, 1766 to September 24, 1766.

Major-General Guy Carleton was appointed Lt.-Governor on April 7, 1766. He began his term as Governor on October 26, 1768 and left for England in 1770 to lobby for changes in the government.

Hector C. Cramahé, Dean of the Council, was chosen Administrator on August 9, 1770, when Carleton left for England. He became Lt.-Governor on September 26, 1771.

Governor Carleton returned in September, 1774, bringing with him the Quebec Act, which had been passed on June 22, 1774. This Act extended the boundaries of Quebec to include land south of Lake Erie to the Ohio River, west to the Mississippi, and north to Rupert's Land which belonged to the Hudson's Bay Company. Labrador was also added to Quebec.

Ethan Allen and Benedict Arnold captured Ticonderoga for the Americans on May 10, 1775, and Crown Point on May 12, 1775. Carleton proclaimed martial law on June 9, 1775, suspending the administrative provisions of the Quebec Act. Richard Montgomery captured Montreal on November 13, 1775, but failed to take Quebec on December 31, 1775, and was killed there.

Civil jurisdiction was re-established in the district of Quebec on July 23, 1776. Carleton resigned on June 26, 1777, but remained in command until June 27, 1778.

Lt.-General Sir Frederick Haldimand was appointed Governor on June 27, 1778, and held office until April 22, 1786.

Henry Hamilton served as Lt.-Governor from June 24, 1782 to November 2, 1785.

Brigadier-General Henry Hope was Lt.-Governor from November 2, 1785 to April 13, 1789. He died in office.

By the definitive Treaty of Paris of September 3, 1783, which ended the Revolutionary War, the land south of the Great Lakes to the Ohio River, west to the Mississippi River, north to Lake of the Woods and east to Lake Superior was ceded to the United States.

Guy Carleton was again named Commander-in-Chief in Canada on February 23, 1782. He was made Governor of British North America on April 11, 1786; his powers now extended over Quebec, Nova Scotia, New Brunswick, St. John's Island and Newfoundland. He became Baron, Lord Dorchester on August 21, 1786.

Major-General Allured Clarke was appointed Lt.-Governor on March 19, 1790, with his term beginning on October 8, 1790.

The Constitutional Act of 1791, passed on June 19, 1791, established representative government in Canada. The Act did not divide Canada, but assumed that a division would take place. The Governor acted with the advice and consent of the legislative council and an assembly in each of the two provinces. The council was to be summoned under the great seal of the province, membership was to be for life. The Governor appointed and he could remove the speaker of the council. The King was to authorize the Governor to call the assembly. Parliament was to be summoned once every twelve months, not to continue for more than four years; the Governor could dissolve it at any time.

Dorchester left for England on August 18, 1791, leaving

Clarke to administer the government.

By Order-in-Council, August 24, 1791, the Province of Quebec was divided into: Upper Canada (Ontario) with a temporary capital at Newark (Niagara-on-the-Lake); and Lower Canada (Quebec) with its capital at Quebec City.

November 18, 1791. Clarke issued a proclamation declaring that the Constitutional Act of 1791 was to go into effect on December 26, 1791.

Governors of Lower Canada 1791-1841

Lord Dorchester was again appointed Governor-in-Chief of Upper and Lower Canada in September, 1791. His term of office began December 26, 1791 when the provisions of the Constitutional Act of 1791 went into effect. He returned to Quebec on September, 1793 and served until December 15, 1796. He died November 10, 1808.

Allured Clarke was appointed Lt.-Governor of Lower Canada September 12, 1791, to be effective when the Constitutional Act of 1791 came into force, and he served until January 21, 1796.

The first Parliament of Lower Canada convened on December 17, 1792. Jean Antoine Panet was elected as its first Speaker.

Robert Prescott began his term as Lt.-Governor on June 21, 1796. He acted as Administrator from July 12, 1796, and held office as Governor from April 27, 1797 to August 29, 1807. However, he returned to England on July 30, 1799, leaving the office in the hands of Administrators.

Sir Robert Shore Milnes was appointed Administrator on November 4, 1797. He served from July 30, 1799 to August 12, 1805, with his term ending on November 29, 1808.

Thomas Dunn. President of the Council. Acted again as Administrator from August 12, 1805 to October 24, 1807.

General Sir James Henry Craig began his term as Governor on October 24, 1807. He resigned on June 19, 1811 and died on January 12, 1812.

Sir Francis Burton was named Lt.-Governor on November 29, 1808. By now this position was a sinecure since the Governor confined his activities almost exclusively to Lower Canada. The Lieutenant-Governor of Upper Canada, nominally under the authority of the Governor worked independently, for all practical purposes.

Thomas Dunn. President of the Council. Acted as Administrator from June 19, 1811 to September 14, 1811.

Sir George Prevost acted as Administrator from September 14, 1811 to July 15, 1812.

Major-General Isaac Brock, Commander of Forces, was appointed Administrator April 9, 1812, but he did not act in this capacity.

General Sir George Prevost began his term as Governor on July 15, 1812 and served until April 4, 1815.

Francis, Baron de Rottenberg, President of the Council, acted as Administrator from February 20, 1813 to March 16, 1813; and from May 12, 1813 to June 14, 1813.

George Glasgow, President of the Council, acted as Administrator from June 14, 1813 to September 25, 1813.

Francis, Baron de Rottenberg, President of the Council, again acted as Administrator from October 11, 1814 to November 30, 1814.

The War of 1812 was declared by the United States on June 18, 1812. Americans under General Wade Hampton were defeated on the Chateauguay River, on October 25, 1813, by French Canadians under Colonel Charles de Salaberry. At the naval battle of Plattsburgh, Lake Champlain, on September 11, 1814, the Americans, under Commodore Thomas Macdonough, defeated the British under Captain Downie. Governor Prevost was turned back at this point.

The Treaty of Ghent, ending the war, which was signed on December 24, 1814, and was ratified by the United States Senate on February 18, 1815, restored the status quo ante bellum. The boundary west from Lake of the Woods was to remain unsurveyed beyond the point at which it intersected latitude 49° north.

Lt.-General Sir Gordon Drummond was Administrator from April 4, 1815 to May 21, 1816.

John Wilson was Administrator from May 21, 1816 to July

12, 1816.

General Sir John C. Sherbrooke's term as Governor extended from July 12, 1816 to July 30, 1818.

The Assembly was given control over ordinary expenditures in 1818.

Charles Lennox, 4th Duke of Richmond was Governor from July 30, 1818 to August 28, 1819; he died in office.

James Monk, President of the Council, acted as Administrator from August 20, 1818 to March 17, 1820.

Sir Peregrine Maitland, who was Lt.-Governor of Upper Canada from 1818-1828, acted as Administrator from March 17, 1820 to June 19, 1820.

George Ramsay, Earl of Dalhousie, was Governor from June 19, 1820 to September 8, 1828. He was appointed Commander-in-Chief of India in 1828.

Sir Francis Burton, Lt.-Governor, acted as Administrator from June 7, 1824 to September 16, 1825.

Lt.-General Sir James Kempt acted as Administrator from September 8, 1828 to October 20, 1830.

General Matthew Whitworth, 5th Baron Aylmer, acted as Administrator from October 20, 1830 to February 4, 1831. His term as Governor extended from February 4, 1831 to August 24, 1835.

Archibald Acheson, 2nd Earl of Gosford, was Governor from August 24, 1835 to March 30, 1838. He was also Chief Commissioner of the three commissioners sent to ascertain the state of the province. The others were Sir George Gipps and Sir Charles Grey. The assembly, which was dominated by the French, wanted more power in government and an elected legislative council. The Parliament was prorogued on August 26, 1837, and it never reassembled under the Constitution of 1791.

The Rebellion of 1837 in Lower Canada began on November 6, 1837 in Montreal, and it collapsed on December 13, 1837 in St. Eustache. Louis Papineau, the chief instigator of the rebellion, fled to the United States.

On February 10, 1838, an Act to Make Temporary Provision for the Government of Lower Canada was passed. The Constitution of 1791 was suspended from the date of proclamation of this Act until November 1, 1840. The Governor was to set up a special council, to make laws which were limited in operation. This Special Council continued until November 1, 1842.

Chairmen of the Special Council of Lower Canada during the suspension of the Constitution of 1791 were:

James Cuthbert, from April 18, 1838 to June 1, 1838.

Toussaint Pothier, from November 5, 1838 to November 11, 1839.

Chief Justice James Stuart, from November 11, 1839 to January 28, 1841.

George Moffatt, from January 28, 1841 to February 10, 1841.

Sir John Colborne acted as Administrator from February 27, 1838 to May 29, 1838.

John George Lambton, Earl of Durham, was appointed Governor-in-Chief of all British North America Provinces except Newfoundland, and High Commissioner for Upper and Lower Canada, on April 24, 1838.

He arrived in Canada on May 29, 1838. His mission was to discover causes of unrest and to make recommendations for providing a more tranquil government in Canada.

The Earl of Durham left for England on November 1, 1838. His report, laid before Parliament February 11, 1839, supplied materials for the legislation between 1839-1841 on which modern Canadian progress is founded. He advocated a legislative union between Upper and Lower Canada, and prescribed colonial self-government.

Sir John Colborne acted as Administrator from November 1, 1838 to January 17, 1839. His term as governor extended from January 17, 1839 to October 19, 1839.

Charles Poulette Thomson, Viscount Sydenham, was Governor from October 19, 1839 to February 5, 1841. He was sent to promote a union of Upper and Lower Canada; to reconcile differences

31

between the legislature, the people and the Home government, and to establish the administrative machinery for a new government.

Lieutenant-Governors of Upper Canada 1792-1841

John Graves Simcoe was Lt.-Governor from July 8, 1792 to April 10, 1796.

On September 17, 1792, he convened the first legislature of Upper Canada, at Newark (Niagara-on-the-Lake), the temporary capital.

On August 26, 1793, he established the first permanent capital on the site of an abandoned French fur-trading post at Toronto, renaming it York.

Peter Russell, President of the Council, acted as Administrator from July 20, 1796 to August 17, 1799.

Major-General Peter Hunter was Lt.-Governor from August 17, 1799 to August 21, 1805, when he died in office.

Alexander Grant, President of the Council, acted as Administrator from September 11, 1805 to August 25, 1806.

Francis Gore was Lt.-Governor from August 25, 1806 to January 1, 1818, but he took a leave of absence from October 9, 1811 to September 21, 1815.

Major-General Isaac Brock, Commander of Forces, acted as Administrator from October 9, 1811 to October 13, 1812. He prorogued the Assembly, and declared martial law, on July, 1812. Brock took Detroit from the Americans under General William Hull, August 16, 1812, but was killed at Queenston, on the Niagara River, on October 13, 1812, when repulsing the Americans under General Stephen Van Rensselaer.

Sir Roger H. Sheaffe, Commander of Forces, acted as Administrator from October 12, 1812 to June 19, 1813.

Francis, Baron de Rottenburg, President of the Council, acted as Administrator from June 19, 1813 to December 13, 1813.

At the battle of Lundy's Lane on July 24, 1813, the British under General Gordon Drummond, fought the fiercest battle of the war, against the Americans under General Jacob Brown, but results were inconclusive.

On September 13, 1813, the Americans, under Captain Oliver H. Perry, defeated the British, under Captain Robert Barclay at the naval battle of Put-in-Bay on Lake Erie.

On October 5, 1813, the Americans, under General William H. Harrison, defeated the British, under Colonel Henry Proctor, at the Battle of the Thames near Moraviantown. Tecumseh, the Shawnee chief, was killed at this battle. Newark was burned by the Americans, under Major-General McClure, on December 12, 1813.

Major-General Gordon Drummond, Commander of Forces, acted as Administrator from December 13, 1813 to April 25, 1815.

Buffalo was burned by the British under Major-General Riall, on December 29, 1813.

York was captured, and the parliament buildings were burned by the Americans, under Major-General Henry Dearborn, on April 27, 1814. Colonel Zebulon Pike died in this battle.

The seat of government was moved to Kingston.

The British, under Colonel Robert McDouall, occupied Prairie du Chien on July 18, 1814.

Sir George Murray was Provisional Lieutenant-Governor from April 25, 1815 to July 1, 1815.

Sir Fred Philpse Robinson was Provisional Lieutenant-Governor from July 1, 1815 to September 21, 1815.

Lt.-Governor Gore resumed authority on September 21, 1815, and his term ended on January 6, 1818.

Samuel Smith acted as Administrator from June 11, 1817 to August 13, 1818.

Sir Peregrine Maitland was Lt.-Governor from August 13, 1818 to August 23, 1828.

Sir John Colborne was Lt.-Governor from November 4, 1828 to November 30, 1835.

The Welland Canal was opened to ships between Lake Erie and Lake Ontario in 1829.

Full control of the whole revenue was granted to the Assembly in 1831.

Rideau Canal between Bytown (Ottawa) and Kingston was completed 1832.

33

The name of York was changed to Toronto in 1834.

Colborne assumed the military command of British North America January 26, 1836.

Sir Francis B. Head was Lt.-Governor from January 25, 1836 to March 23, 1838.

The rebellion of 1837 in Upper Canada began on December 5, 1837 in Toronto, and collapsed there on December 7, 1837. William Lyon Mackenzie, chief instigator of the rebellion, fled to the United States.

Sir George Arthur was Lt.-Governor from March 23, 1838 to February 5, 1841, the last Lieutenant-Governor of Upper Canada under the Constitution of 1791.

Governors-General of United Canada   1839-1867

The Act of Union, was passed on July 23, 1840, and became effective on February 5, 1841. It united the Provinces of Upper and Lower Canada. Upper Canada (Ontario) became Canada West; Lower Canada (Quebec) became Canada East. This Act provided for an elective assembly and a legislative council appointed for life or good behavior. A Governor-General appointed by the Crown was the royal representative in the united provinces.

Charles Poulette Thomson, Viscount Sydenham was Governor-General from February 5, 1841 to September 19, 1841, when he died in office. He chose Kingston as the capital of the United Provinces on February 10, 1841.

Robert Baldwin (Reform-West) and William Draper (Conservative-East) were appointed to form a coalition ministry. Baldwin resigned just before the first parliament opened June 14, 1841, leaving Draper to carry on the government.

Sir Richard D. Jackson was Administrator from 1841 to 1842.

Sir Charles Bagot was Governor-General from January 12, 1842 to May 19, 1843, when he died in office.

Parliament was convened on September 8, 1842, and Draper resigned on September 14, 1842.

Baldwin (Reform-West) and Louis H. LaFontaine (Reform-East) organized a ministry on September 26, 1842.

Sir Charles Theophilus, Lord Metcalfe was Governor-General from March 30, 1843 to November 26, 1845.

Parliament convened in September 1843. The Baldwin-La Fontaine ministry resigned on November 26, 1843 and Dominic Daly (E) formed a care-taker ministry.

The capital was moved from Kingston to Montreal on May 10, 1844.

William Draper (W) and Denis B. Viger (E) organized a conservative ministry on December 12, 1844. Viger resigned on June 17, 1845 and his place was taken by Louis Papineau.

Charles Murray Cathcart, 2nd Earl of Cathcart was appointed Governor-General in 1846. He had acted as Administrator from November 26, 1845 to April 24, 1846, and his term as Governor-General extended from April 24, 1846 to January 30, 1847.

The Oregon boundary dispute was settled on June 15, 1846.

James, 8th Earl of Elgin and Kincardine was Governor-General from January 30, 1847 to December 19, 1854. He allowed the colony complete self-government in domestic affairs and was the last Governor-General to rule as well as to reign.

Draper (W) resigned May 28, 1847 and his place was taken by Henry Sherwood.

On December 6, 1847, the Assembly was dissolved by Lord Elgin.

The election went against the ministry, it resigned on a vote of no confidence. The Robert Baldwin (W)--Louis H. LaFontaine (E) reform ministry was organized on March 11, 1848. This was the first real cabinet in Canada and it marked the beginning of responsible government.

The Tories in Montreal revolted against passage of the Rebellion Losses Bill. The parliament building was burned and Lord Elgin was castigated by the mob. As a compromise, it was decided to have the Assembly meet alternately in Toronto and Quebec. Under this arrangement, Toronto was the seat of government from November 14, 1849; Quebec from September 22, 1851.

Sir Francis Hincks (W) and Augustín N. Morin (E) organized a liberal ministry on October 28, 1851; Hincks resigned on September 10, 1854 and his place was taken by Sir Alan N. MacNab. Morin resigned on December 19, 1854.

Sir Edmund Walker Head was Governor-General from December 19, 1854 to October 25, 1861.

Sir Alan N. MacNab (W) and Sir Étienne P. Taché (E) set up a Liberal-Conservative ministry on January 27, 1855. The capital was at Toronto from October 20, 1855 to September 24, 1859. MacNab resigned on May 23, 1856 and his place was taken by John Alexander Macdonald.

The Legislative Council (upper house) was made elective in 1856.

Taché resigned on November 25, 1857 and his place was taken by Sir George E. Cartier.

George Brown (W) and Sir Antoine A. Dorion (E) formed a Liberal ministry on August 2, 1858.

Sir George E. Cartier (E) and John Alexander Macdonald (W) formed a Liberal-Conservative ministry on August 6, 1858.

Charles Stanley Monck, 4th Viscount Monck was Governor-General 1861-1867. He had acted as Administrator from October 25, 1861 to November 28, 1861, and his term as Governor-General extended from November 28, 1861 to June 30, 1867.

John Sandfield Macdonald (W) and Louis Sicotte (E) formed a ministry on May 24, 1862. Sicotte resigned on May 15, 1863 and his place was taken by Antoine A. Dorion.

The Conservative ministry of Sir Étienne P. Taché (E) and John Alexander Macdonald (W) began on March 30, 1864. They resigned on June 14, 1864, and reorganized on June 18, 1864. They secured the cooperation of George Brown and the Liberals by pledging to work for a federation of Canada East, Canada West, the Maritime Provinces and the North West Territories.

Meanwhile, a conference had been called by the Maritime Provinces to meet in Charlottetown, Prince Edward Island, on September 1, 1864, to discuss a legislative union of Nova Scotia, New Brunswick and Prince Edward Island. Canada obtained permission to attend to consider federation of all the provinces. The resulting talks were favorable, and another meeting was called to meet in Quebec, October 10, 1864.

At the Quebec Conference, with Sir Étienne P. Taché as chairman, seventy-two resolutions were agreed upon as the basis for action. These were to be presented to the various provinces for ratification and to the national Parliament for enactment. These resolutions formed the basis of the British North America Act of 1867, the constitution under which Canada still functions.

Taché died on July 29, 1865. The Conservative ministry of John Alexander Macdonald (Canada West) and Sir Narcisse Belleau (Canada East) took office on August 7, 1865 as a caretaker ministry to await the outcome of the dominion negotiations.

<u>Prime Ministers of Canada 1867-</u>

The British North American Act became law on March 28, 1867. Imperial Order-in-Council, May 22, 1867, declared that the three Provinces of Nova Scotia, New Brunswick and Canada, the last now to be divided into Ontario and Quebec, would be united on July 1, 1867 as the Dominion of Canada. In addition to providing for the government of the named provinces, it prescribed procedures by which future provinces would be admitted into the Dominion. The capital of the Dominion was to be at Ottawa.

John Alexander Macdonald, the first Prime Minister of the Dominion of Canada was a conservative. His tenure was from July 1, 1867 to November 5, 1873.

The first parliament of the Dominion met in November, 1867.

On July 15, 1870, Manitoba came into the Dominion as the 5th Province.

On July 15, 1870, Rupert's Land, which formerly belonged to the Hudson's Bay Company, came under the jurisdiction of the Dominion government, as the North West Territories.

On July 20, 1871, British Columbia came into the Dominion as the 6th Province.

On July 1, 1873, Prince Edward Island came into the Dominion as the 7th Province.

Alexander Mackenzie, a Liberal, succeeded John A. Macdonald on November 7, 1873, and he served until October 16, 1878.

John Alexander Macdonald regained the post of Prime Minister on October 17, 1878. He died in office on June 6, 1891.

On July 31, 1880, all British possessions in North America except Newfoundland were annexed to the Dominion. This applied particularly to the Arctic regions, which had heretofore been outside of any territorial jurisdiction.

On November 7, 1885, the Canadian Pacific Railroad was completed at Craigellachie, British Columbia.

Sir J. C. Abbott, Conservative, June 16, 1891 to November 24, 1892.

Sir John S. D. Thompson, Conservative, December 5, 1892 to December 12, 1894.

Sir Mackenzie Bowell, Conservative, December 21, 1894 to April 27, 1896.

Sir Charles Tupper, Conservative, May 1, 1896 to July 8, 1896.

Sir Wilfrid Laurier, Liberal, July 11, 1896 to October 6, 1911.

On September 1, 1905, Alberta and Saskatchewan came into the Dominion as the 8th and 9th Provinces.

Sir Robert Laird Borden, Conservative, October 10, 1911 to July 10, 1920.

Arthur Meighen, Conservative, July 10, 1920 to December 29, 1921.

William Lyon Mackenzie King, Liberal, December 29, 1921 to June 28, 1926.

Arthur Meighen, Conservative, retook the office from June 29, 1926 to September 25, 1926.

William Lyon Mackenzie King, Liberal, regained the position on September 25, 1926, and held it until August 6, 1930.

Richard B. Bennett, Viscount Bennett, Conservative, August 7, 1930 to October 23, 1935.

William Lyon Mackenzie King, Liberal, became Prime
Minister for the third time and served from October 23, 1935
to November 15, 1948.

Louis Stephen St. Laurent, Liberal, from November 15,
1948 to June 21, 1957.

On April 1, 1949, Newfoundland came into the Dominion
as the tenth Province.

John G. Diefenbaker, Conservative, served from June
21, 1957 to April 23, 1963.

Lester Pearson, Liberal, took office on April 22, 1963.

Pierre E. Trudeau, Liberal, took office on April 20,
1968.

Governors-General of the Dominion of Canada 1867-

Charles Stanley Monck, 4th Viscount Monck, was appointed
on June 1, 1867, and inaugurated on July 1, 1867.

The last Governor-General of United Canada, continued
on as the first Governor-General of the Dominion of Canada.

John Young, Baron Lisgar, was appointed on December
29, 1868, and inaugurated on February 2, 1869.

Frederick T. H. Blackwood, Earl of Dufferin, was appointed on May 22, 1872, and inaugurated on June 25, 1872.

John D. S. Campbell, Marquis of Lorne, was appointed
on October 5, 1878, and inaugurated on November 25, 1878.

Henry C. K. Petty-Fitzmaurice, 5th Marquis of Lands-
downe, was appointed on August 18, 1883, and inaugurated on
October 23, 1883.

Frederick A. Stanley, 16th Earl of Derby, was appointed
on May 1, 1888, and inaugurated on June 11, 1888.

John C. H. Gordon, 1st Marquis of Aberdeen, was appointed on May 22, 1893, and inaugurated on September 18, 1893.

Gilbert John E. M. Kynynmond, 4th Earl of Minto, was
appointed on July 30, 1898, and inaugurated on November 12, 1898.

Albert H. G. Grey, 4th Earl Grey, was appointed on
September 26, 1904, and inaugurated on December 10, 1904.

H.R.H. Albert, Duke of Connaught, was appointed on March

21, 1911, and inaugurated October 13, 1911.

Victor C. W. Cavendish, 9th Duke of Devonshire, was appointed on August 19, 1916, and inaugurated on November 11, 1916.

Julian H. G. Byng, 1st Viscount Byng of Vimy, was appointed on August 2, 1921, and inaugurated on August 11, 1921.

Freeman Freeman-Thomas, Viscount Willingdon, was appointed on August 5, 1926, and inaugurated on October 2, 1926.

Vere Brabazon Ponsonby, Earl of Bessborough, was appointed on February 9, 1931, and inaugurated on April 4, 1931.

John Buchan, 1st Baron Tweedsmuir, was appointed on August 10, 1935, and inaugurated on November 2, 1935.

1st Earl of Athlone, Prince Alexander of Teck, was appointed on April 3, 1940, and inaugurated on June 21, 1940.

Harold Alexander, 1st Viscount Alexander of Tunis, was appointed on August 1, 1945, and inaugurated on April 12, 1946.

Vincent Massey, was appointed on January 24, 1952, and inaugurated on February 28, 1952.

Major-General George P. Vanier, was appointed on August 1, 1959, and inaugurated on September 15, 1959. He died in office on March 5, 1967.

Roland Michener was appointed on March 25, 1967 and inaugurated on April 17, 1967.

Quebec: Lieutenant-Governors 1867-

Sir Narcisse F. Belleau was commissioned July 1, 1867.

René Caron was commissioned February 11, 1873.

Luc Lettelier de Saint-Just was commissioned December 15, 1876.

Theodore Robitaille was commissioned July 26, 1879.

L. F. R. Masson was commissioned on October 4, 1884.

Auguste-Réal Angers was commissioned on October 24, 1887.

Sir Joseph-Adolphe Chapleau was commissioned on December 5, 1892.

Sir Louis-Amable Jette was commissioned on January 20, 1898.

Sir Charles A. Pelletier was commissioned on September 15, 1908.

Sir François Langelier was commissioned on May 5, 1911.

Sir Pierre-Evariste Leblanc was commissioned on February 9, 1915.

Sir Charles Fitzpatrick was commissioned on October 21, 1918.

Louis-Philippe Brodeur was commissioned on October 31, 1923.

Narcisse Pérodeau was commissioned on January 8, 1924.

Sir Lomer Gouin was commissioned on December 31, 1928.

Henry George Carroll was commissioned on April 2, 1929.

E. L. Patenaude was commissioned on April 29, 1934.

Maj.-General Sir Eugene Fiset was commissioned on December 30, 1939.

Gaspard Fautex was commissioned on October 3, 1950.

Onesime Gagnon was commissioned on February 14, 1958.

Paul Comtois was commissioned on October 6, 1961.

Hughes Lapointe was commissioned on February 22, 1966.

Quebec: Premiers 1867-

Pierre J. O. Chauveau, Conservative, was appointed July 15, 1867.

Gédéon Ouimet, Conservative, was appointed February 27, 1873.

Charles Boucher, Conservative, was appointed September 22, 1874.

Henri Joly, Liberal, was appointed March 8, 1878.

Joseph-Adolphe Chapleau, Conservative, was appointed October 31, 1879.

J.-Alfred Mousseau, Conservative, was appointed August 1, 1882.

John J. Ross, Conservative, was appointed January 23, 1884.

L.-Olivier Taillon, Conservative, was appointed January 13, 1887.

Honore Mercier, Liberal, was appointed January 29, 1887.

Charles Boucher, Conservative, was appointed December 21, 1891.

L.-Olivier Taillon, Conservative, was appointed December 16, 1892.

Edmund J. Flynn, Conservative, was appointed May 11, 1896.

F.-Gabriel Marchand, Liberal, was appointed May 24, 1897.

S.-Napoleon Parent, Liberal, was appointed October 3, 1900.

Sir Lomer Gouin, Liberal, was appointed March 23, 1905.

L.-Alexandre Taschereau, Liberal, was appointed July 9, 1920.

Adelard Godbout, Liberal, was appointed June 11, 1936.

Maurice Duplessis, Union Nationale, was appointed August 24, 1936.

Adelard Godbout, Liberal, was appointed November 8, 1939.

Maurice Duplessis, Union Nationale, was appointed August 30, 1944.

Jean-Paul Sauve, Union Nationale, was appointed September 10, 1959.

Antonio Barrette, Union Nationale, was appointed January 7, 1960.

Jean Lesage, Liberal, was appointed July 5, 1960.

Daniel Johnson, was appointed June 16, 1966.

Ontario: Lieutenant-Governors 1867-

Major-General H. W. Stisted was commissioned on July 1, 1867.

W. P. Howland was commissioned on July 14, 1868.

John W. Crawford was commissioned on November 5, 1873.

D. A. Macdonald was commissioned on May 18, 1875.

John B. Robinson was commissioned on June 30, 1880.

Sir Alexander Campbell was commissioned on February 8, 1887.

Sir George A. Kirkpatrick was commissioned on May 28, 1892.

Sir Oliver Mowat was commissioned on November 18, 1897.

Sir William M. Clark was commissioned on April 20, 1903.

Sir John M. Gibson was commissioned on September 22, 1908.

Lt. -Colonel John S. Hendrie was commissioned on September 26, 1914.

Lionel H. Clarke was commissioned on November 27, 1919.

Colonel Henry Cockshutt was commissioned on September 10, 1921.

William D. Ross was commissioned on December 20, 1926.

Colonel Herbert A. Bruce was commissioned on October 25, 1932.

Albert Matthews was commissioned on November 23, 1937.

Ray Lawson was commissioned on December 26, 1946.

Louis O. Breithaupt was commissioned on January 24, 1952.

John K. Mackay was commissioned on December 30, 1957.

William E. Rowe was commissioned on March 1, 1963.

Ontario: Premiers 1867-

John S. Macdonald, Conservative, was appointed on July 16, 1867.

Edward Blake, Liberal, was appointed on December 20, 1871.

Oliver Mowat, Liberal, was appointed on October 25, 1872.

A. S. Hardy, Liberal, was appointed on July 25, 1896.

G. W. Ross, Liberal, was appointed on October 21, 1899.

Sir J. P. Whitney, Conservative, was appointed on February 8, 1905.

Sir William Hearst, Conservative, was appointed on October 2, 1914.

E. G. Drury, United Farmers, was appointed on November 14, 1919.

G. H. Ferguson, Conservative, was appointed on July 16, 1923.

G. S. Henry, Conservative, was appointed on December 15, 1930.

M. F. Hepburn, Liberal, was appointed on July 10, 1934.

G. D. Conant, Liberal, was appointed on October 21, 1942.

H. C. Nixon, Liberal, was appointed on May 18, 1943.

George Drew, Conservative, was appointed on August 17, 1943.

T. L. Kennedy, Conservative, was appointed on October 19, 1948.

Leslie M. Frost, Conservative, was appointed on May 4, 1949.

John P. Robarts, Conservative, was appointed on November 8, 1961.

ACADIE - NOVA SCOTIA

Originally, Acadie included Nova Scotia, New Brunswick, Cape Breton Island, the Gaspé peninsula and northern Maine. The name Acadie came into general use after 1604.

Pierre du Guast, Sieur de Monts, was named Lieutenant-General in Acadie, November 8, 1603, by Henry IV. He granted the area of Port Royal, now Annapolis, to Jean de Biencourt, Sieur de Poutrincourt, in 1604, but retained the remainder of his grant. Made a settlement on the St. Croix River, in what is now Maine, and wintered there 1604-1605. He then moved his colony to Port Royal in the summer of 1605. Poutrincourt took over the command on July 27, 1605, his grant having been confirmed by the King.

DeMonts, his trading concession having been cancelled, turned his attention to the St. Lawrence Valley. In 1611 he ceded the remainder of his rights in Acadie to Antoinette de Pons, Marquise de Guercheville, wife of the Duc de la Rochefoucauld-Liancourt. She put Captain LaSaussaye in charge of an expedition which founded a Jesuit mission on St. Sauveur (Mount Desert Island), May 21, 1613. The mission was razed by Samuel Argall, an adventurer under orders from Sir Thomas Dale, Governor of Virginia, in October, 1613. Madame de Guercheville surrendered her rights in Acadie to Richelieu's Company of New France when it was organized on April 29, 1627.

Jean de Biencourt, Sieur de Poutrincourt took command of the Port Royal area on July 27, 1605. He made several trips back and forth between Port Royal and France. He had left his son Charles de Biencourt in charge at Port Royal and was in France when Samuel Argall razed the colony in November, 1613. When he returned to Port Royal on May 27, 1614, and discovered the damage, he built a small house, turned it over to his son and left Acadie for the last time. He was killed in battle at Méry-sur-Seine, December 15, 1615.

44

Charles de Biencourt, son and heir of Poutrincourt and owner of Port Royal, died in Acadie in 1624, designating Charles de la Tour as his heir. LaTour abandoned Port Royal, and settled a post called Fort Laméron, on Cape Sable, renaming it Fort Saint Louis.

On September 10, 1621, James I of England, made a grant which included Nova Scotia, New Brunswick and the Gaspé peninsula, to Sir William Alexander, a Scots nobleman. He gave the name Nova Scotia (New Scotland) to the area. The first attempt at settlement, in the winter of 1621-1622, failed.

On June 25, 1625, Alexander received authorization from Charles I to create baronetcies in Nova Scotia.

In 1627, settlers disembarked at abandoned Port Royal, and erected a post called Scots Fort or Charles Fort.

On February 4, 1629, Sir William Alexander and David Kirke--the conqueror of Quebec--received a charter from Charles I to form the Anglo-Scotch Company, with a monopoly of trade in the whole country.

Claude Turgis de la Tour, was captured by the English, in June, 1628 and taken to England. When he was returned to Acadie, he persuaded his son Charles to join him. On October 6, 1629, at Charles Fort, the two of them came to terms with Alexander's son, also named William, who granted them all of Acadie from Cape Fourchu (Yarmouth) to Port Mirligouéchel (Lunenburg). The La-Tours both renounced their French citizenship and became English subjects. In the fall, young Alexander took Claude to England, where Sir William Alexander made him a baronet of Nova Scotia, on November 30, 1629. On April 30, 1630, Sir William granted a baronetcy each to the LaTours, Claude accepting for himself and for his son. On May 12, 1630, Sir William approved Charles as a baron of Nova Scotia.

Back in Acadie, Charles learned that Acadie would be returned to France. He repudiated his agreement with Alexander, and accepted a commission from Louis XIII, dated February 8, 1631, as Lieutenant-General of the Fort Saint Louis region.

Isaac de Razilly was appointed Lieutenant-General for the

entire province of Acadie on March 10, 1632, by Louis XIII.

The Treaty of St. Germaine-en-Laye, March 23, 1632, restored Acadie to the French, and on April 20, 1632, Razilly was appointed Lieutenant-General of all New France, i.e., Quebec, Acadie and Newfoundland. Thus, Champlain at Quebec and LaTour at Fort St. Louis were nominally under his command; however Razilly confined his actions to Acadie, leaving Champlain undisturbed at Quebec. As his base, he started a settlement at LeHavre on September 8, 1632, naming it Port Ste. Marie-de-Grace. Razilly received the surrender of Acadie from the English, under Captain Andrew Forester, at Charles Fort (Port Royal) in December, 1632. He died November, 1635.

Charles de Menou, Sieur d'Aulnay-Charisnay and Charles Amador de la Tour were joint Lieutenant-Generals after the death of Razilly; both were responsible to the One Hundred Associates for the operation of the fur trade and to the King for administration.

A letter from Louis XIII, on February 10, 1638, defined the limits of their jurisdictions: d'Aulnay-Charisnay was to command from Chignecto Bay westward to Pentagoet; de la Tour to command from Chignecto Bay eastward to Cape Canso. D'Aulnay maintained his bases at Le Havre and Port Royal; LaTour at Fort St. Louis and Fort St. John. Eventually civil war broke out between the two. LaTour was recalled to France February 13, 1641 and his commission was annulled on February 23, 1641.

Charles de Menou, Sieur d'Aulnay-Charisnay was appointed Commander over the territory formerly belonging to LaTour, on March 2, 1641. On August 22, 1641, d'Aulnay occupied Fort St. Louis and burned it. LaTour retired to Fort St. John, and refused to report to the King. He finally left the country. D'Aulnay was appointed Governor over all Acadie, February, 1647, with powers which superceded the claims of the One Hundred Associates. He drowned on May 24, 1650.

Charles de la Tour was relieved of all charges against him on February 16, 1651, and was appointed Governor and Lieutenant-General of Acadie on February 25, 1651. The ownership of the country was restored to the One Hundred Associates. LaTour arrived at Fort St. John on September 23, 1651, and set up residence there. He married Jeanne Matin, widow of d'Aulnay, in July, 1653. Their marriage contract was dated February 24, 1653.

The English under Robert Sedgewick captured Fort St. John, on July 27, 1654, and LaTour was taken to London. He sold his interest in Acadie to William Crowne and Sir Thomas Temple, fur-traders, on September 20, 1656 and returned to Acadie where he died in 1663.

Sir Thomas Temple was appointed Governor by Oliver Cromwell. He was appointed a baronet in Nova Scotia in 1662.

Acadie was returned to the French again by the Treaty of Breda, on July 31, 1667, but it was not occupied by them until 1670, whereupon Temple's commission lapsed.

Hector d'Andigne, Sieur de Grandfontaine was Governor from 1670 to 1673; his commission dated March 6, 1670.

On July 6, 1670, in Boston, d'Andigne signed a treaty of restitution with Sir Thomas Temple, restoring Acadie to the French. He became Governor on August 5, 1670, when Captain Richard Walker handed Pentagouët over; the transfer was completed on September 2, 1670, when Port Royal was surrendered. Governor d'Andigne made his residence at Pentagouët (Penobscot). The first census was taken in 1671.

Captain Jacques de Chambly was appointed Commander in Acadie on May 5, 1673, subject to the Governor of Canada. He was appointed Governor in 1676.

He was captured by the buccaneer, Juranien Aernauts on August 10, 1674 and was carried to Boston. After being ransomed by Frontenac, Governor of Quebec, he returned to Acadie, and made his capital at Port Royal. In 1677, he was appointed Governor of Grenada.

Pierre de Joibert, Sieur de Marson was temporary Commander during 1678; he died in office.

Lt. Michel le Neuf de la Vallière was appointed interim commander in 1678, by Frontenac, Governor of Quebec. He was officially appointed Governor August 5, 1683 and served until 1684.

François Marie Perrot was appointed Governor on April 10,

1684, and was dismissed in March, 1687.

Louis Alexander des Friches, Chevalier de Menneval was appointed Governor on March 1, 1687 and served until 1690.

He surrendered to New Englanders, under Sir William Phipps, who occupied Port Royal May 20, 1690 and was taken to Boston as a prisoner. First Sergeant Chevalier was left in charge.

Captain Joseph Robineau, Sieur de Villebon was appointed interim Governor in April, 1691, and served as Governor until 1700. He captured the vessel bringing Colonel Edward Tyng, the newly appointed British Governor to Acadie. When he recaptured Port Royal on November 27, 1691, he reclaimed Acadie for France.

Acadie was restored to the French by the Treaty of Ryswick on September 20, 1697. Governor Villebon died in office July 5, 1700.

Lieutenant de Villieu was temporary Commander from 1700 to 1701.

Jacques François de Brouillan was appointed Commander of Acadie, arriving June 29, 1701. He was given the title of Governor in 1702. He went to France on December 18, 1704, but died on shipboard, in Halifax Bay on September 22, 1705, when returning to Acadie.

Simon Denys de Bonaventure was Administrator from 1704 to 1706.

Daniel d'Auger, Sieur de Subercase was appointed Governor on April 10, 1706. He was the last French Governor of Acadie.

Port Royal surrendered to the British, under Colonel Francis Nicholson, on October 13, 1710. This was during the War of the Spanish Succession (Queen Anne's War in the Colonies). Port Royal was renamed Annapolis Royal.

By the Peace of Utrecht, on April 11, 1713, the French lost Acadie and Newfoundland permanently, but retained Ile Royale (Cape Breton Island) and Ile Saint Jean (St. John's Island, which later became Prince Edward Island).

English Governors of Nova Scotia

Samuel Vetch was appointed Governor by Colonel Nicholson

when Port Royal (Annapolis Royal) was captured on October 13, 1710.

Col. Francis Nicholson was appointed Governor on October 20, 1712, and arrived in 1714.

Thomas Caulfield was appointed Lieutenant-Governor to act in the absence of Governor Nicholson.

Samuel Vetch was again named Governor on January 20, 1715, and held the office until 1717, even though he did not return to Nova Scotia. Affairs were administered by Thomas Caulfield, Lt.-Governor who died in office on March 2, 1717.

Col. Richard Philipps was appointed Governor on August 17, 1717. He was appointed Captain-General and Commander-in-Chief on July 9, 1719, and served until 1749. He died October 15, 1750, in London.

Colonel of the 40th Regiment, a small garrison in Annapolis Royal, Philipps resided mostly in London, administering personally only from April 25, 1720 to October, 1723, and from June, 1729 to August 27, 1731; however, he drew his salary as Governor until 1749. Regimental officers were appointed as Lieutenant-Governors to administer the colony. The senior officer at Annapolis was made Lieutenant-Governor of the garrison.

Captain John Doucett was appointed Lt.-Governor of the fort and garrison at Annapolis on May 25, 1717. He died on November 19, 1726.

Major Lawrence Armstrong was appointed Lt.-Governor of Nova Scotia on February 8, 1725. He arrived May 29, 1725, and died on December 6, 1739.

Colonel Alexander Cosby was named Lt.-Governor of the fort and garrison of Annapolis. He took office on October 20, 1727, died December 27, 1742.

John Adams was Administrator of the area from 1739 to 1740.

As senior councillor present in the colony when Lt.-Governor Armstrong died, he took command on December 7, 1739.

Major Paul Mascarene, was senior councillor, but had been absent in Boston when Armstrong died. He took command as President of the Council on March 22, 1740.

49

France declared war on England on March 15, 1744 n.s., beginning the War of the Austrian Succession. From August 24 to September 25, 1744, Mascarene withstood an attack on Annapolis led by du Vivier from Louisbourg. After this action, Mascarene was appointed Lieutenant-Governor of the fort of Annapolis, which office he held until July, 1750, when he was relieved by Major Charles Lawrence. Mascarene died in 1760.

Colonel Edward Cornwallis was appointed Governor on May 9, 1749, and he also served as Captain-General. Cornwallis arrived on June 21, 1749, at Chebucto (Halifax harbor), and took command from Mascarene on July 13, 1749.

Halifax was settled in July, 1749 and the seat of government was moved there from Annapolis Royal. Halifax became the center of commercial activity of British North America.

Peregrine Thomas Hopson was inaugurated as Governor on August 3, 1752. He came from Cape Breton Island when Louisburg was restored to the French. Hopson left for England on November 1, 1753, for his health, but he did not resign his commission until January 7, 1756.

By act of Parliament, the old style Julian calendar was changed to the new style Gregorian calendar in Great Britain and her colonies. To make this change, the day after September 2, 1752 was designated September 14, 1752.

Fort St. John fell to the British under General Moncton on June 21, 1755. This was the last French fort in Acadie.

Colonel Charles Lawrence administered for Hopson from November 1, 1753 as Lieutenant-Governor. He was appointed Governor and Captain-General on December 8, 1755 and began his term on July 23, 1756. He died in office on October 19, 1760.

Acadians were deported on orders promulgated on July 28, 1755, by Lawrence's Council. The deportation was carried out from September to December, 1955, by Captain James Murray and New England soldiers.

A Legislative Assembly, the first popularly elected parliament in British North America, convened at Halifax on October 2, 1758. Robert Sanderson was its Speaker. The Government of the colony then consisted of three parts: 1) the Governor was head

50

of the colonial administration; 2) the Council, nominated by the Governor and appointed for life by the Crown, was the executive council of the governor, the upper house of the legislature and the highest judicial body; and 3) the House of Assembly, which was elected by the property owners, had the power to vote appropriations for support of local government. It did not control the casual, territorial or crown revenues.

On August 17, 1759, the Governor and Council divided the province into the five counties of Annapolis, Kings, Cumberland, Lunenburg and Halifax.

Henry Ellis was appointed Governor in April, 1761 and the Assembly was notified of his appointment on July 24, 1761. He never came to Nova Scotia and resigned in October 1763.

Jonathan Belcher, Chief Justice, acted as Administrator after the death of Lawrence. He took office as Lieutenant-Governor November 21, 1761 and served until 1763.

Colonel Montague Wilmot took office as Lieutenant-Governor on September 26, 1763. He was appointed Governor and Captain-General on October 8, 1763. Wilmot died in office on May 23, 1766.

On October 7, 1763, by Royal Proclamation, St. John's Island and Cape Breton Island were annexed to the government of Nova Scotia.

Benjamin Green took command as Administrator at the time of Governor Wilmot's death.

Michel Francklin, Lt.-Governor took office as administrator on August 23, 1766.

Lord William Campbell became Governor on November 27, 1766. He was appointed Governor of South Carolina in June, 1773.

Michel Francklin, Lt.-Governor, acted as Administrator from October 1, 1767 to September 10, 1768 and from November 4, 1768 to December 4, 1768.

St. John's Island became a separate colony on June 28, 1769.

Benjamin Green was Administrator from October 17, 1771 to June 1, 1772.

Michel Francklin, Lt.-Governor, acted as Administrator from June 2, 1772 to July 10, 1772. He died on November 8, 1782.

Francis Legge took office as Governor on October 8, 1773. He was recalled and left for England on May 12, 1776, but he drew his salary as Governor until July 29, 1782.

Commodore Marriott Arbuthnot was Lt.-Governor from April 22, 1776; he served as Administrator from May 13, 1776 to August 17, 1778, when he returned to England.

Commissioner Sir Richard Hughes, 2nd Baronet, became Lt.-Governor on August 17, 1778, and served as Administrator from that date to July 31, 1781.

Sir Andrew S. Hammond, 1st Baronet was Lt.-Governor from 1781 to 1782. He took office on July 31, 1781; and served as Administrator from that date to October 18, 1782.

John Parr became Governor on October 19, 1782.

The province of New Brunswick was formed from the northern part of Nova Scotia. It was formally separated from Nova Scotia on August 16, 1784, and was put under a Governor. Cape Breton Island was given a separate local government August 26, 1784, under the supervision of a Lieutenant-Governor who reported to the government of Nova Scotia.

Prince Edward Island was re-annexed to Nova Scotia on September 11, 1784, and was given a separate local government under a Lieutenant-Governor who reported to the government of Nova Scotia. Prince Edward Island was again separated from Nova Scotia on May 20, 1786.

On April 11, 1786, Lord Dorchester was made Governor-in-Chief of British North America. On May 20, 1786, Parr's title was changed to Lieutenant-Governor, but he continued as head of the government of Nova Scotia until he died in office on November 25, 1791.

Edmund Fanning became Lt.-Governor on September 23, 1783. He held office until May 20, 1786, when Parr's title was changed to Lieutenant-Governor. Fanning then was named Lieutenant-Governor of St. John's Island.

Richard Bulkeley, President of the Council, took command at the death of Parr and served as Administrator from 1791-1792.

Sir John Wentworth took office as Lt.-Governor on May 14, 1791 and served until 1808.

Sir George Prevost, 1st Baronet, was Lt.-Governor from April 13, 1808, until he was transferred to Quebec as Governor of Canada on August 25, 1811.

Alexander Croke, President of the Council, served as Administrator in 1811.

Sir John C. Sherbrooke was Lt.-Governor from October 16, 1811 to June 27, 1816. He was transferred to Quebec as Governor of Canada.

Major-General George Strachey Smith was Administrator in 1816.

George Ramsey, Earl of Dalhousie, was Lt.-Governor from October 24, 1816 to June 1, 1820, when he was transferred to Quebec as Governor of Canada.

Sir James Kempt was Lt.-Governor from June 1, 1820 to August 23, 1828. He then transferred to Quebec as Governor of Canada.

Cape Breton Island was re-annexed to Nova Scotia, under a proclamation by Lt.-Governor Kempt on October 9, 1820.

Michel Wallace was Administrator in 1828.

Sir Peregrine Maitland was Lt.-Governor from November 28, 1828 to January 24, 1834.

Thomas N. Jeffrey was Administrator from 1832 to 1834.

Sir Colin Campbell was Lt.-Governor from July 2, 1834 to September 29, 1840.

The Assembly was dissolved on November, 1836. The Reform Party, led by Joseph Howe, won the election. The new Assembly was convened on January 31, 1837.

Lucius Cary, 10th Viscount Falkland was Lt.-Governor from September 30, 1840 to August 2, 1846.

The Council was organized on September 30, 1840 and Simon Bradstreet Robie, Conservative, was elected President. The real head of the Council was James W. Johnston.

Parliament was dissolved on October 21, 1840. The Liberals won the election, and the new Assembly met on February 3, 1841. Joseph Howe was elected Speaker. This resulted in a coalition government, with the Liberals controlling the Assembly, and the Conservatives controlling the Council. Howe resigned the Speakership on January 26, 1843, and William Young, Conservative, became Speaker.

Sir Jeremiah Dickson was Administrator in 1846.

Sir John Harvey was Lt.-Governor from August 29, 1846 to March 22, 1852.

The election of August 5, 1847 was a victory for the Liberals. The Assembly convened on January 25, 1848 with William Young as Speaker. The Conservative Council resigned January 27, 1848 on a vote of no confidence from the Assembly.

A Liberal Council took office on February 9, 1848. James B. Uniacke, President of the Council (upper house) of the first responsible government, was the nominal head or premier, although he held the portfolio of attorney general.

John Bazalgette was Administrator in 1852.

Sir John Gaspard LeMarchant was Lt.-Governor from August 5, 1852 to February 15, 1858.

William Young's Liberal ministry took office on April 4, 1854.

James W. Johnston's Conservative ministry took office on February 24, 1857.

George Phipps, Earl of Mulgrave, was Lt.-Governor from February 15, 1858 to September 17, 1863.

William Young's Liberal ministry began on February 10, 1860.

Joseph Howe's Liberal ministry began on August 3, 1860.

James W. Johnston's Conservative ministry took over on June 11, 1863.

Charles Hastings Doyle was Administrator from 1863 to 1864.

Charles Tupper's Conservative ministry began May 11, 1864.

Sir Richard Graves MacDonnell was Lt.-Governor from June

22, 1864 to September 28, 1865.

Charles Hastings Doyle was Administrator in 1865.

Sir William F. Williams was Lt.-Governor from November 8, 1865 to June 30, 1867, when Nova Scotia came into the Dominion of Canada as one of the four original provinces. Dr. Charles Tupper was Premier of the Confederate (Conservative) ministry when this event occurred.

Lieutenant-Governors 1867-

Lt.-General Sir William F. Williams. Commissioned July 1, 1867.

Lt.-General Sir C. Hastings Doyle. Commissioned October 18, 1867.

Joseph Howe. Commissioned May 1, 1873.

Sir Adam G. Archibald. Commissioned July 4, 1873.

Matthew H. Richey. Commissioned July 4, 1883.

A. W. McLelan. Commissioned July 9, 1888.

Sir Malachy B. Daly. Commissioned July 11, 1890.

Alfred G. Jones. Commissioned July 26, 1900.

Duncan C. Fraser. Commissioned March 27, 1906.

James D. McGregor. Commissioned October 18, 1910.

David MacKeen. Commissioned October 19, 1915.

MacCallum Grant. Commissioned November 29, 1916.

J. Robson Douglas. Commissioned January 12, 1925.

James C. Tory. Commissioned September 14, 1925.

Frank Starfield. Commissioned November 19, 1930.

Walter H. Covert. Commissioned October 5, 1931.

Robert Irwin. Commissioned April 7, 1937.

Frederick F. Mathers. Commissioned May 31, 1940.

Lt.-Colonel Ernest Kendall. Commissioned November 17, 1942.

J. A. D. McCurdy. Commissioned August 12, 1947.

Alistair Fraser. Commissioned September 1, 1952.

Maj.-General Edward C. Plow. Commissioned January 15, 1958.

H. P. MacKeen. Commissioned March 1, 1963.

Premiers 1867-

H. Blanchard. Conservative. Appointed July 4, 1867.

William Annand. Liberal. Appointed November 7, 1867.

P. C. Hill. Liberal. Appointed May 11, 1875.

S. H. Holmes. Conservative. Appointed October 22, 1878.

J. S. D. Thompson. Conservative. Appointed May 25, 1882.

W. T. Pipes. Liberal. Appointed August 3, 1882.

W. S. Fielding. Liberal. Appointed July 28, 1884.

George H. Murray. Liberal. Appointed July 20, 1896.

E. H. Armstrong. Liberal. Appointed January 24, 1923.

E. N. Rhodes. Conservative. Appointed July 16, 1925.

Col. Gordon S. Harrington. Conservative. Appointed August 11, 1930.

Angus L. Macdonald. Liberal. Appointed September 5, 1933.

A. S. MacMillan. Liberal. Appointed July 10, 1940.

Angus L. Macdonald. Liberal. Appointed September 8, 1945.

Harold Connolly. Liberal. Appointed April 13, 1954.

Henry D. Hicks. Liberal. Appointed September 30, 1954.

Robert L. Stanford. Conservative. Appointed November 20, 1956.

George I. Smith. Appointed September 13, 1967.

NEW BRUNSWICK

New Brunswick separated from Nova Scotia on August 16, 1784. It was made a province, with a nominated council acting as executive and legislature and an elected assembly. The first capital was located at St. John.

Governors 1784-1867

Colonel Thomas Carleton was appointed Governor on August 16, 1784. His term began on November 22, 1784. When his brother, Sir Guy Carleton, Lord Dorchester, was named Governor-in-Chief of British North America, his title was changed to Lt.-Governor, May 20, 1786. Col. Carleton retired to England on October 4, 1803, but held the title of Lt.-Governor until he died, February 27, 1817. During his absence, the government was administered by the President of the Council.

In November, 1785, the abandoned Acadian settlement of St. Anne's Point was selected by Carleton to be the site of Fredericton, his capital. The first government convened there on July 18, 1788.

Gabriel G. Ludlow was Administrator from October 5, 1803 to February 12, 1808.

Edward Winslow was Administrator from February 20, 1808 to May 23, 1808.

Martin Hunter was Administrator from May 24, 1808 to December 16, 1808.

George Johnstone was Administrator from December 17, 1808 to April 27, 1809.

Martin Hunter was again Administrator from April 28, 1809 to September 10, 1811.

William Balfour was Administrator from September 11, 1811 to November 13, 1811.

Martin Hunter was Administrator, for the third time, from November 14, 1811 to June 14, 1812.

George Stracey Smyth was Administrator from June 15, 1812 to August 16, 1813.

Sir Thomas Saumarez was Administrator from August 17, 1813 to August 13, 1814.

George Stracey Smyth was Administrator a second time, from August 14, 1814 to June 24, 1816.

Harris W. Hailes was Administrator from June 25, 1816 to June 30, 1817.

George Stracey Smyth was Lt.-Governor from July 1, 1817 to March 27, 1823, when he died in office.

Ward Chipman, President of the Council, administered from April 1, 1823 to February 9, 1824.

James Murray Bliss, President of the Council, administered from February 21, 1824 to August 27, 1824.

Sir Howard Douglas, 3rd Baronet, was Lt.-Governor from August 28, 1824 to July, 1831.

William Black, President of the Council, administered from March 30, 1829 to September 8, 1831.

Sir Archibald Campbell, Baronet, was Lt.-Governor from September 9, 1831 to March 28, 1837.

By a Royal Commission, November 20, 1832, New Brunswick was given two distinct councils: one entirely executive (later the cabinet), and one entirely legislative (upper house).

Sir John Harvey was Lt.-Governor from March 29, 1837 to April 25, 1841, when he was re-assigned to Newfoundland.

Sir William Colebrook was Lt.-Governor from April 26, 1841 to April 10, 1848.

The Webster-Ashburton Treaty, August 9, 1842, settled the Maine-New Brunswick boundary.

Sir Edmund Walker Head was Lt.-Governor from April 11, 1848 to September 28, 1854. He was re-assigned as Governor-General of Canada, and later became Governor of the Hudson's Bay Company.

Sir John H. T. Manners-Sutton, Viscount Canterbury, was Lt.-Governor from October 7, 1854 to October 25, 1861.

Election of October, 1854, resulted in a Liberal victory.

Charles Fisher, who was recognized as the Liberal leader, was appointed attorney-general in the Executive Council and was asked to form a government that would have the confidence of the Legislative Assembly. The Assembly which convened November 1, 1854 was considered to be the beginning of responsible government in New Brunswick. The Fisher ministry resigned May 22, 1856, in a disagreement with the Lieutenant-Governor over temperance.

Edward B. Chandler was the leader of the Conservative Party and was a member of the Legislative Council. He formed a ministry upon Fisher's resignation. His ministry was sustained by an election and a new assembly which convened in special session on July 17, 1856. The election of May, 1857 yielded inconclusive results, so the Chandler ministry resigned.

Charles Fisher again formed a Liberal ministry upon the resignation of Chandler. He was discharged from the Executive Council by the Lieutenant-Governor, on a charge of improper purchase of Crown lands on March 18, 1861.

Samuel L. Tilley, formed a Liberal, pro-Confederation, ministry upon the resignation of Fisher.

Sir Arthur Hamilton Gordon, 1st Baron Stanmore, was Lt.-Governor from October 26, 1861 to September 30, 1866.

The Tilley ministry was defeated in the election of March, 1865, over the issue of confederation.

Albert J. Smith formed an anti-Confederation ministry as a result of the election of March, 1865. He resigned on April 10, 1866, under pressure from the Legislative Council, on the issue of confederation.

Peter Mitchell formed a pro-Confederation ministry on April 14, 1866. It was sustained in the election of May 25-June 12, 1866.

Sir Charles Hastings Doyle was Administrator from October 1, 1866 to June 30, 1867.

On July 1, 1867, the Mitchell ministry negotiated the entrance of New Brunswick into the Dominion of Canada as one of the original Provinces. Mitchell was chosen by Samuel Tilley for a cabinet position in John Alexander Macdonald's first ministry of the Dominion government.

Lieutenant-Governors 1867-

Maj.-General Sir Charles H. Doyle. Commissioned July 1, 1867.

Col. F. P. Harding. Commissioned October 18, 1867.

Lemuel A. Wilmot. Commissioned July 14, 1868.

Samuel L. Tilley. Commissioned November 5, 1873.

E. Barron Chandler. Commissioned July 16, 1878.

Robert D. Wilmot. Commissioned February 11, 1880.

Sir Samuel L. Tilley (again). Commissioned October 31, 1885.

John Boyd. Commissioned September 21, 1893.

John A. Fraser. Commissioned December 20, 1893.

A. R. McClelan. Commissioned December 9, 1896.

Jabez B. Snowball. Commissioned January 30, 1902.

L. J. Tweedie. Commissioned March 2, 1907.

Josiah Wood. Commissioned March 6, 1912.

G. W. Ganong. Commissioned June 29, 1916.

William Pugsley. Commissioned November 6, 1917.

William F. Todd. Commissioned February 24, 1923.

Maj.-General Hugh H. McLean. Commissioned December 11, 1928.

Colonel Murray MacLaren. Commissioned February 5, 1935.

W. G. Clark. Commissioned March 5, 1940.

David L. MacLaren. Commissioned November 1, 1945.

J. Leonard O'Brien. Commissioned June 6, 1958.

John B. McNair. Commissioned June 9, 1965.

Premiers 1867-

A. R. Wetmore. Conservative. Appointed 1867.

G. E. King. Liberal. Appointed 1872.

J. J. Fraser. Conservative. Appointed 1878.

D. L. Hannington. Conservative. Appointed 1882.

A. G. Blair. Liberal. Appointed 1883.

James Mitchell. Conservative. Appointed July, 1896.

H. R. Emerson. Liberal. Appointed October 29, 1897.

L. J. Tweedie. Conservative. Appointed August 31, 1900.

William Pugsley. Liberal. Appointed March 6, 1907.

C. W. Robinson. Liberal. Appointed May 31, 1907.

J. D. Hazen. Conservative. Appointed March 24, 1908.

James K. Flemming. Conservative. Appointed October 16, 1911.

George G. Clarke. Conservative. Appointed December 17, 1914.

James Murray. Conservative. Appointed February 1, 1917.

Walter E. Foster. Liberal. Appointed April 4, 1917.

Peter Veniot. Liberal. Appointed February 28, 1923.

John B. M. Baxter. Conservative. Appointed September 14, 1925.

Charles D. Richards. Conservative. Appointed May 19, 1931.

L. P. D. Tilley. Conservative. Appointed June 1, 1933.

A. Allison Dysart. Liberal. Appointed July 16, 1935.

J. B. McNair. Liberal. Appointed March 13, 1940.

H. J. Fleming. Conservative. Appointed October 8, 1952.

Louis J. Robichand. Liberal. Appointed July 12, 1960.

ILE SAINT JEAN-ST. JOHN'S ISLAND-PRINCE EDWARD ISLAND

The French Regime   1534-1763

The Indians called the island Abegweit, "Rocked in the Waves."

Jacques Cartier sighted the island on June 29, 1534, and explored the north and west shores, from June 30 to July 1, 1534, before going on to Gaspé.

The Company of New France, or the One Hundred Associates was chartered by Cardinal Richelieu on April 29, 1627. It gained ownership of the island until February 24, 1663, when its rights were reconveyed to the Crown.

On December 3, 1653, Sieur Nicolas Denys received, as a grant from the Company of New France, part of Acadie which included Ile Saint Jean and Ile Royale. The grant was confirmed on January 30, 1654 by Louis XIV, who named Denys Governor and Lieutenant-General.

He settled at Saint Pierre, on Ile Royale, where he had previously built a fort and had been evicted by agents of the widow of d'Aulnay-Charisney. He made no settlement on Ile Saint Jean, as required by the terms of his grant and various parts of his domain were granted to others.

On January 19, 1663, Sieur François Doublet received a grant from the Company of New France which included Ile Saint Jean. He was to make a settlement in return for the fishing privileges. When he died in 1664, his company disintegrated.

In May, 1686, Sieur Gabriel Gautier received a grant which included Ile Saint Jean and Ile Royale. In return for the privilege of establishing a shore fishery, he was to pay one-half marc of silver each year. His company failed.

In 1710, Sieur de Louvigny was granted the entire eastern coast to a depth of six leagues. By the Royal Edict of July 6, 1711, he was required to make a settlement within a year or lose his concession.

The island was kept by the French after the Peace of Utrecht, on April 11, 1713.

De Louvigny's concession was cancelled in May, 1716, and Ile Saint Jean was re-united with the Royal Domain.

In August, 1719, Comte de Saint Pierre was granted the Ile Saint Jean by the Duke of Orleans, regent during the minority of Louis XV. His grant was to be under the authority of Louisbourg, Ile Royale. On January 18, 1720, Saint Pierre received the Magdalen and Brion Island also. He was to found settlements and build roads.

Sieur de Gotteville de Belle Isle was appointed Commandant by Saint Pierre on March 9, 1721. He served until 1722.

In the summer of 1720, de Gotteville, assisted by Denys de la Ronde, made a settlement at Port la Joie, as the capital. The first white settlement on the island, it remained the capital to the end of the French Regime. De Gotteville retired in 1722 because of ill health.

Sieur du Bois Berthelot de Beaucours was appointed Commandant on February 3, 1722 by Saint Pierre, to succeed de Gotteville. He returned to Ile Royale in 1723, to serve as Lieutenant de Roi.

Sieur Robert Poitier du Buisson was appointed Sub-Delegate of the Intendente of New France on March 10, 1722 by the King. He was responsible for fiscal and judicial administration until he died in office in March, 1744.

The Company which Saint Pierre headed became bankrupt, and the settlers dispersed by the end of 1723. Saint Pierre's rights to exclusive fishing were revoked on October 23, 1725, and his title to the island was revoked by decree of June 1, 1730.

Joseph de Pensens was appointed Commandant on July 2, 1726, by Saint Ovide de Brouillan, Governor of Ile Royale. He was to re-assert French claims to the island and to rally the scattered settlers. On June 2, 1733, he was appointed Lieutenant de Roi. He moved to Louisbourg in 1736, and retired April 2, 1737.

On July 17, 1731, a grant was signed by Louis XV to the Company of the East (Compagnie de l'Ile Saint Jean), of which Jean

Paul de Roma was Director. He was ceded the area around present Trois Rivières and set up a feudal estate, which paid homage to Louisbourg. Justice was to be administered by the Sub-Delegate of the Intendente of Ile Saint Jean.

In June, 1732, Roma arrived at Trois Rivières, and chose Brudenell Point as the site of his estate. In May, 1737, he bought out the other partners and was appointed Commandant of Trois Rivières, to be under orders from Louisbourg.

du Haget was acting Commandant at Port la Joie from the time de Pensen left until the arrival of the incoming Commandant.

Louis du Pont de Chambon was appointed Lieutenant de Roi on May 17, 1737, and his command was separate from that of the garrison.

In the Spring of 1744, when the War of the Austrian Succession broke out in Europe, the news reached Louisbourg May 3, 1744, and du Chambon left to become Administrator of Ile Royale. The Intendente, du Buisson, having died in March, 1744, the island was left without Governor or Intendente, When Du Chambon went to Ile Royale, in the autumn of 1744, Du Vivier was put in charge of a garrison of twenty soldiers.

On June 17, 1745, Louisbourg fell to the British and New Englanders. When Trois Rivières was destroyed on June 20, 1745, Roma escaped to Quebec. When Port la Joie was destroyed, du Vivier and the garrison escaped to Quebec, and Ile Saint Jean was governed from Louisbourg.

On September 30, 1745, Admiral Warren, Commander at Louisbourg, promised the inhabitants of Ile Saint Jean that they would not be molested, provided that they remain neutral. On June 9, 1746, the indulgence was extended by Commodore Charles Knowles, Warren's successor at Louisbourg.

In September, 1748, Captain Benoit was sent by la Galis-sonière, Administrator of New France, to be in charge of a garrison at Port la Joie.

On October 18, 1748, Ile Saint Jean and Ile Royale were returned to the French by the Treaty of Aix-la-Chapelle.

On July 3, 1749, Louisbourg was evacuated by the British

and the French took possession.

Sieur Denis de Bonnaventure was appointed Commandant in August, 1749. He was transferred to Louisbourg in April, 1754. He re-established the capital at Port la Joie, still subject to the orders of the Governor of Louisbourg. Acadians began immigration to Ile Saint Jean after the British evacuated Louisbourg.

François Marie Goutin was appointed Sub-Delegate of the Intendente of New France in August, 1749. He died in office in 1752, and the office was not filled after his death.

Rosseau de Villejouin was appointed Commandant in April, 1754.

On July 26, 1758, the British, under General Amherst, gained control of Louisbourg, and with it, Ile Saint Jean.

British Military Occupation 1758-1763

On August 8, 1758, Colonel, Lord Rollo was instructed by General Amherst to proceed to Saint John's Island and inform the inhabitants of the fall of Louisbourg.

Rollo arrived on the island on the same day, and began the first fortification on the island, which he called Fort Amherst. Some 3500 inhabitants were deported to France, leaving an estimated 300 in isolated parts of the island. Commander Villejouin was sent to England as a prisoner. He was the last French Commander of Ile Saint Jean.

Lord Rollo returned to Louisbourg on November 14, 1758, and Captain Johnston was left in charge of a garrison of 190 men from Brigg's Regiment. Every spring a new detachment relieved the old.

Captain Adlam was Commander from 1759 to 1760, in charge of 180 men from the 40th Regiment.

Captain Hill was Commander 1760-1762. He was in charge of 160 men from the 22nd and 45th Regiments from 1760 to 1761, and 117 men from the same regiments from 1761 to 1762.

Captain Sinclair was Commander from 1762 to 1763. He was in charge of a detachment from the 45th Regiment.

Captain Hill was Commander 1763-1764. He was in charge

of two companies, about 110 men.

The British Regime 1763-1851

The island was ceded permanently to the British by the Treaty of Paris on February 10, 1763, and it was placed under the government of Nova Scotia by the Proclamation of 1763 on October 7, 1763.

In May, 1768, Michael Francklin, Lieutenant-Governor of Nova Scotia and his Council divided the island into the three counties: King's, Queen's, and Prince. The site of Charlottetown was selected as the capital by Francklin and Captain Samuel Holland, Canada's first surveyor. The site selected was across the harbor from Port la Joie.

On June 22, 1768, a government was instituted by the opening of a Court of Common Pleas and General Sessions.

Michael Francklin was appointed Lt.-Governor on August 13, 1768.

An Order-in-Council, on June 28, 1769, gave the island, under the name of St. John's Island, a separate government. Executive and legislative functions were placed under a Governor and an appointed Council.

Walter Patterson was named Captain-General and Governor on August 4, 1769. He began active duty September 29, 1770. He was in England from 1775 to 1780 and Philipps Callbeck, Attorney-General in the Council, served as Administrator during this period. Callbeck was captured by the Americans on December 8, 1775, but returned to his office in 1776.

Thomas DesBrisey was Lt.-Governor from 1769 to 1786, but he spent little time in the colony.

On September 11, 1784, St. John's Island was re-annexed to Nova Scotia. Governor Parr of Nova Scotia was named Captain General and Governor of Nova Scotia, St. John's Island and Cape Breton Island. Patterson's commission as Governor was revoked and reissued naming him Lieutenant-Governor of St. John's Island. Governor Parr's authority was to be exercised only when he was physically present on the island, at other times Patterson was in

66

command.

On May 20, 1786, St. John's Island separated from Nova Scotia, and it again became a separate province. Patterson continued as Lieutenant-Governor, now under Lord Dorchester (Guy Carleton) who was Governor-in-Chief at Quebec.

Edmund Fanning was appointed Lieutenant-Governor on June 30, 1786. He had formerly been Lieutenant-Governor of Nova Scotia. Fanning arrived November 4, 1786, but Governor Patterson refused to give up the office until his dismissal letter arrived from London, in May, 1787. The island had two Governors for this period.

The first elected Assembly convened on July 7, 1793. The Council then assumed two functions. As the Legislative Council, it was presided over by the Chief Justice and acted as the upper house of the legislature; as the Executive Council it was presided over by the Lieutenant-Governor and acted as his cabinet. The same people composed both councils.

On February 1, 1799, the name of the island was changed to Prince Edward Island, after H.R.H. Prince Edward, third son of George III, at that time Commander-in-Chief of British Forces in Canada. Prince Edward later became Duke of Kent and, later, the father of Queen Victoria. The change in name was confirmed by the King in Council on the above date.

Joseph F.W. Des Barres was Lt.-Governor from May 10, 1804 to August 4, 1812. He had been Lieutenant-Governor of Cape Breton Island.

Charles Douglas Smith was Lt.-Governor from August 5, 1812 to April 18, 1824.

Lt.-Colonel John Ready was Lt.-Governor from April 19, 1824 to March 15, 1831.

Annual legislative sessions were instituted in 1825.

Sir Murray Maxwell was Lt.-Governor from March 16, 1831 to July 25, 1831.

Sir Aretas W. Young was Lt.-Governor from July 26, 1831 to December 1, 1835. He died in office.

George Wright was Administrator from 1835 to 1836. He

was a surveyor.

Sir John Harvey was Lt.-Governor from August 30, 1836 to March 30, 1837. He was re-assigned to New Brunswick.

Sir Charles A. Fitzroy was Lt.-Governor from March 31, 1837 to November 2, 1841.

On March 4, 1839, a proclamation by the Lieutenant-Governor, separated the Executive and the Legislative Councils. This was authorized in instructions from Sir John Colborne, Governor-in-Chief of Canada dated December 13, 1838.

George Wright was Administrator in 1841. He was a surveyor.

Sir Henry Vere Huntley was Lt.-Governor from November 13, 1841 to November 1, 1847.

Sir Donald Campbell, Baronet, was Lt.-Governor from December 9, 1847 to October 10, 1850. He died in office.

Ambrose Lane, Senior Councillor, was Administrator from 1850 to 1851.

Sir Alexander Bannerman was Lt.-Governor from March 10, 1851 to July 11, 1854.

On April 24, 1851, George Coles, leader of the Reform (Liberal) party, advised the Assembly that he had been asked by the Lieutenant-Governor to form a government which would have the confidence of the assembly. This announcement signified the beginning of responsible government in Prince Edward Island, and Coles, in effect, became the first premier.

Responsible Government 1851-1873

Lieutenant-Governors

Sir Dominique Daly was Lt.-Governor from July 11, 1854 to May 25, 1859.

Charles Young, President of the Legislative Council, was Administrator from May 25, 1859 to June 8, 1859.

George Dundas was Lt.-Governor from June 8, 1859 to October 22, 1868.

Sir Robert Hodgson, Chief Justice, was Administrator from
October 22, 1868 to October 6, 1870.

William C. F. Robinson was Lt.-Governor from October 6, 1870,
to June 10, 1873.

Premiers

George Coles. Liberal. Appointed 1851.

John Holl. Conservative. Appointed 1854.

George Coles. (again). Liberal. Appointed 1855.

Edward Palmer. Conservative. Appointed 1859.

On December 2, 1862, the Act to make the Legislative
Council elective went into effect.

Colonel John H. Gray. Conservative. Appointed 1863.

On September 1, 1864, delegates from Nova Scotia, New
Brunswick and Prince Edward Island assembled at Charlottetown to
discuss a legislative union of the three provinces.   They were
joined the same day by delegates from Canada East and Canada
West to discuss a plan of Confederation of the combined provinces.
From this conference and the subsequent one at Quebec which
convened October 10, 1864, emerged the Dominion of Canada.

James C. Pope. Conservative. Appointed 1865.

George Coles. (third time). Liberal. Appointed 1867.

Joseph Hensley. Liberal. Appointed 1869.

Robert P. Haythorne. Liberal. Appointed 1869.

James C. Pope. (again). Conservative. Appointed 1870.

Robert P. Haythorne (again). Liberal. Appointed 1871.

The last Premier to sit in the Legislative Council, was
James C. Pope (third time). Conservative. 1873.

By Imperial Order-in-Council, June 26, 1873, to be effective July 1, 1873, Prince Edward Island was admitted into the
Dominion of Canada as the 7th Province.

Lieutenant-Governors 1873-

William Robinson. Commissioned June 10, 1873.

Sir Robert Hodgson. Commissioned July 4, 1874.

Thomas H. Haviland. Commissioned July 10, 1879.

Andrew A. Macdonald. Commissioned July 18, 1884.

Jedediah S. Carvell. Commissioned September 2, 1889.

George W. Howlen. Commissioned February 21, 1894.

P. A. McIntyre. Commissioned May 23, 1899.

D. A. MacKinnon. Commissioned October 3, 1904.

Benjamin Rogers. Commissioned June 1, 1910.

A. C. Macdonald. Commissioned June 3, 1915.

Murdoch MacKinnon. Commissioned September 2, 1919.

Frank R. Heartz. Commissioned September 8, 1924.

Charles Dalton. Commissioned November 19, 1930.

George D. DeBlois. Commissioned December 28, 1933.

Bradford W. LePage. Commissioned September 11, 1939.

J. A. Bernard. Commissioned May 18, 1945.

T. W. L. Prowse. Commissioned October 4, 1950.

F. Walter Hyndman. Commissioned March 31, 1958.

W. J. Macdonald. Commissioned August 1, 1963.

Premiers 1867-

James C. Pope. Conservative. Appointed April, 1873.

L. C. Owen. Conservative. Appointed September, 1873.

L. H. Davies. Conservative. Appointed August, 1876.

W. W. Sullivan. Conservative. Appointed April 25, 1879.

N. McLeod. Conservative. Appointed November, 1889.

F. Peters. Liberal. Appointed April 27, 1891.

A. B. Warburton. Liberal. Appointed October, 1897.

D. Farquharson. Liberal. Appointed August, 1898.

A. Peters. Liberal. Appointed December 29, 1901.

F. L. Haszard. Liberal. Appointed February 1, 1908.

H. James Palmer. Liberal. Appointed May 16, 1911.

John A. Mathieson. Conservative. Appointed December 2, 1911.

Aubin Arsenault. Conservative. Appointed June 21, 1917.

J. H. Bell. Liberal. Appointed September 9, 1919.

James D. Stewart. Conservative. Appointed September 5, 1923.

Albert C. Saunders. Liberal. Appointed August 12, 1927.

Walter M. Lea. Liberal. Appointed May 20, 1930.

James D. Stewart (again). Conservative. Appointed August 29, 1931.

William J. P. MacMillan. Conservative. Appointed October 14, 1933.

Walter M. Lea (again). Liberal. Appointed August 15, 1935.

Thane A. Campbell. Liberal. Appointed January 14, 1936.

J. Walter Jones. Liberal. Appointed May 11, 1943.

A. W. Matheson. Liberal. Appointed May 25, 1953.

Walter R. Shaw. Conservative. Appointed September 1, 1959.

ILE ROYALE - CAPE BRETON ISLAND

On November 8, 1621, Robert Gordon of Lochinvar received a grant from Charles I, of the Barony of Galloway, which included Cape Breton Island, the Gulf Islands and the north shore of Acadie. Lord Ochiltree, a Lieutenant of Gordon, started a settlement at Port-aux-Baleines in June, 1629. He was taken prisoner by the French under Captain Daniel on September 18, 1629.

Captain Daniel built a fort at Gran-Cibou, and named it Fort Sainte Anne. He left a garrison of 40 men under Sieur Claude de Beauvais, and took his prisoners to France. The settlement failed.

On the death of Razilly (1636), Nicolas Denys, Sieur de Fronsac, was appointed King's Governor and Lieutenant-General of the whole extent of the Bay of St. Lawrence and the adjacent islands from Cape Canso to Cape Rosiers. He formed settlements at Chedabouctou (Guysborough), Nova Scotia and Saint Pierre, Cape Breton.

On December 3, 1653, he received a grant from the Company of New France that coincided with the territory of which he had been Governor; the grant was confirmed on January 30, 1654, by Louis XIV. Denys was evicted by Emmanuel le Gorgne, creditor of d'Aulnay Charisnay. He went to France where his claim was re-affirmed; later he returned and reclaimed his forts at Saint Pierre and Chedabouctou. He sustained his claim against la Giraudière. When Fort Saint Pierre was burned, sometime before 1672, he retired to Mirimichi in Acadie, where he was still living in 1690. An ordonnance from Duchesneau, Intendant of New France, dated August 21, 1677, recognized and established the right of Denys to levy a duty on coal from Cape Breton and plaster from the Straits of Canso, and to license fur trading within the limits of his grant.

After the death of Denys, Ile Royale came under the jurisdiction of the Governor of Acadie.

Admiral Sir Hovenden Walker took possession of Cape Breton for the British on September 15, 1711, at Spanish River, Baie des Espagnols (Sydney Harbor), during Queen Anne's War.

The island was retained by the French after the Peace of Utrecht on April 11, 1713, which ended Queen Anne's War.

French Governors 1713-1745

When Joseph de Saint-Ovide de Brouillan took possession of Cape Breton on September 2, 1713, in the King's name, he found one Frenchman and 30 Indians on the island. Louisbourg was founded on Havre à l'Anglois, August, 1713, as the first step toward making the island a bastion for the St. Lawrence possessions. Settlement was to be made by displaced French from Placentia, Newfoundland, and from Nova Scotia, both of which were now under British jurisdiction.

Philippe Pasteur de Costabelle was appointed Governor on January 1, 1714. He arrived at Louisbourg on October 2, 1714 and departed for France November 16, 1716, but retained the Governorship until September 21, 1717.

Pierre Auguste de Soubras was appointed Commissaire, on April 1, 1714.

Joseph de Saint Ovide de Brouillan was acting Governor from November 23, 1716 and was appointed Governor on November 16, 1717. He served until 1739.

Jacques Ange le Normant de Mézy was appointed Deputy on April 23, 1718. Sebastien François Ange le Normant de Mézy was appointed Deputy Commissaire on May 1, 1729. He became Commissaire-Ordinaire on January 1, 1733, and Commissaire-Ordonnateur on March 23, 1735.

M. de Bourville was Acting Governor during absences in 1730, 1731, and November, 1737 to 1739.

The fortifications of Louisbourg were begun in 1719.

Isaac-Louis de Forant was appointed Governor on April 1, 1739. He arrived on September 10, 1739, and died in office on May 10, 1740.

François Bigot was appointed Commissaire-Ordinaire on April 1, 1739, and Commissaire-Ordonnateur on March 1, 1741.

M. de Bourville was Administrator from May 10, 1740 to November 2, 1740.

Jean Baptiste Prévost du Quesnal was appointed Governor on September 1, 1740. He arrived on November 2, 1740, and died in office October 9, 1744.

France declared war on England on March 15, 1744 (N.S.) beginning the War of the Austrian Succession (King George's War in the colonies).

Louis Dupont du Chambon was appointed Administrator on October 9, 1744 (N.S.) to June 17, 1745 (O.S.).

Antoine LeMoyne, Sieur de Chateauguay, was appointed Governor on January 1, 1745. Illness prevented him from going to the island, and he died at Rochefort on March 21, 1747.

British Military Governors 1745-1749

Louisbourg was captured by the British and New England militia under Lt.-General Sir William Pepperrell and Admiral Peter Warren. The siege began April 30, 1745, and the fort surrendered June 17, 1745 (O.S.). Commander du Chambon, the garrison and most civilians were sent to Rochefort, France.

Admiral Peter Warren was appointed Acting Governor by Pepperrell when the fort fell, and he became Governor in August, 1745, serving into 1746.

Commodore Charles Knowles was appointed Governor on March 14, 1746. He took office June 2, 1746, and left on November 30, 1747 (O.S.).

Peregrine Thomas Hopson was administrator after the departure of Knowles. He was appointed Governor in the winter of 1748, and departed July 12, 1749 (O.S.).

French Governors 1749-1754

The island was returned to the French by the Treaty of Aix-la-Chapelle, on October 18, 1748, which ended the War of the Austrian Succession.

Captain Charles des Herbiers was appointed Governor on

74

January 1, 1749. He arrived at Louisbourg on June 29, 1749, and took possession for France on July 23, 1749 (N. S.). He left on September 13, 1751.

Jacques Prévost was appointed Commissaire-Ordonnature on January 1, 1749.

Major-General Jean Louis, Comte de Raymond, was appointed Governor on March 1, 1751. He arrived on August 4, 1751, and departed October, 1753.

d'Ailleboust was Administrator from October, 1753 to August 15, 1754.

On May 18, 1756, England declared war on France, beginning the Seven Year's War (French and Indian War in the Colonies).

Augustin, Chevalier Drucour, was appointed Governor 1754-1758. on February 1, 1754, the last French Governor on the island.

On June 8, 1758, the British under brevet-Brigadier General James Wolfe, Admiral Edward Boscawen and General Jeffrey Amherst, Commander-in-Chief, began the attack on Louisbourg. Governor Drucour surrendered July 26, 1758.

British Military Commanders 1758-1763.

Brigadier-General Edward Whitmore was left in charge when General Amherst departed on August 30, 1758. He was later appointed Governor of Louisbourg, Cape Breton Island and St. John's Island by the Imperial Government, serving until 1763.

Lt. -Colonel Tulliken was Commander of the garrison at Louisbourg from 1758 to 1763. The garrison was composed at first of the 22nd, 28th, 40th and 45th Regiments. The garrison, which was later reduced, was housed in buildings of the town, which remained, for a time, the chief settlement on the island.

On February 9, 1760, orders were given by William Pitt, Prime Minister of Great Britain, to destroy the fortifications but not the habitations. The process of demolition took from May 31, 1760 to November 8, 1760, under the direction of Commodore Byron, grandfather of the poet. The garrison remained until 1768.

On February 10, 1763, the Treaty of Paris ended the Seven Year's War. Louisbourg and Cape Breton Island were retained by

Great Britain.

County of Cape Breton 1763-1784

On October 7, 1763 Cape Breton Island was placed under the government of Nova Scotia.

On December 10, 1765 the island was made the county of Cape Breton and was allowed two members in the Assembly of Nova Scotia.

On August 10, 1768, orders were issued to evacuate the garrison.

On August 16, 1768, George Cottnam was appointed Justice of the Peace to keep order and execute the laws when the troops were withdrawn. Cottnam died about October, 1780.

On September 26, 1768, the garrison, now composed of part of the 59th Regiment under Major Milward, was evacuated to Halifax.

Province of Cape Breton 1784-1820

Separated from Nova Scotia August 26, 1784, Cape Breton obtained its own Lieutenant-Governor and Council, subject to orders of the Governor of Nova Scotia, and after May 20, 1786, to those of the Governor-in-Chief at Quebec.

Major Joseph F. W. Des Barres was Lt.-Governor from 1784 to 1787.

Lt.-Colonel William Macarmick was Lt.-Governor from 1787 to 1795.

D. Mathews, Attorney-General, and President of the Council, served as Administrator from May 27, 1795 to June 29, 1798.

Brigadier-General Ogilvie, President of the Council, was Administrator from June 29, 1798 to June 21, 1799.

Brigadier-General Murray was Lt.-Governor from June 21, 1799 to September 16, 1800.

Major-General Despard was Lt.-Governor from September 16, 1800 to July 6, 1807.

Brigadier-General Nepean was Lt.-Governor from July 6,

1807 to June 1, 1813.

Brigadier-General Swayne was Lt.-Governor from January 1, 1813 to February 6, 1816.

Lt.-Colonel Fitzherbert was Lt.-Governor from February 5, 1816 to November 4, 1816.

Major-General Ainslie was Lt.-Governor from November 4, 1816 to June 22, 1820.

Captain David Stewart was Administrator from June 22, 1820 to October 9, 1820.

On October 9, 1820, Cape Breton Island was re-annexed to Nova Scotia, then under the Lieutenant-Governorship of Sir James Kempt, and it has remained a part of that Province to this day.

HUDSON'S BAY COMPANY AND RUPERT'S LAND

Henry Hudson came to James Bay for the Muscovy Company of London, in the Discovery. He wintered at the bottom of James Bay. The crew went ashore on November 2, 1610, and the ship was frozen in by November 10, 1610. When the crew mutinied, Hudson was set adrift on June 21, 1611. His fate is unknown.

Sir Thomas Button came to Canada for the Company of Merchants, Discoverers of the North West Passage. He arrived on August 27, 1612, at the mouth of the Nelson River, which he named, and wintered there.

Médard Chouart des Groseilliers, exploring with his navigator Captain Zechariah Gillam of Boston in the Nonsuch for Prince Rupert and his associates, arrived on September 29, 1668, at the mouth of the Rupert River, named by Gillam. He built Fort Charles and wintered there.

On May 2, 1670, a Charter was signed by King Charles II, to the Governor and Company of Adventurers of England Trading into Hudson's Bay. The affairs of the Company were to be managed by a Governor, Deputy Governor and Committee of seven. The Company was granted the exclusive trade and the mineral and fishing rights in all the lands and waters having access on Hudson's Bay. This area, to be known as Rupert's Land, was finally commonly understood to extend from Labrador to the Rocky Mountains; from the headwaters of the Red River to Chesterfield Inlet. The Company was given the right to make and enforce regulations for the government of the territory and to judge the residents in civil and criminal cases.

Governors of Hudson's Bay Company 1670-1870

Prince Rupert was Governor from 1670 to 1682. He was a cousin of Charles II, third son of Frederick V, King of Bohemia and Elizabeth, granddaughter of Mary, Queen of Scots. He died in office November 29, 1682.

Sir John Robinson, Governor of the Tower of London, was Deputy Governor from 1670 to 1675.

Sir James Hayes, secretary to Prince Rupert, was Deputy Governor from 1675 to 1685.

H. R. H. James, Duke of York, a brother of Charles II, was elected Governor on January 3, 1683, and resigned when he ascended the throne of England as King James II, on February 6, 1685.

John, Baron Churchill, later 1st Duke of Marlborough, was elected Governor on April 2, 1685.

Sir Edward Dering was Deputy Governor from 1685 to 1692.

Under the Treaty of Neutrality with France, on November 19, 1686, at London, all territories were to remain in the hands of the present possessors while commissioners settled disputed boundaries between New France and Rupert's Land.

William and Mary declared war on Louis XIV, on May 7, 1689, beginning King William's War.

Sir Stephen Evans, head of Stephen Evans and Company, bankers, was Governor from 1692 to 1696.

Samuel Clarke, a merchant, was Deputy Governor from 1692 to 1701.

Sir William Trumbull was elected Governor on November 18, 1696. He was Secretary of State during the negotiations leading to the Treaty of Ryswick on September 20, 1697, ending King William's War. By this treaty, possessions of each King were to be restored as they were at the beginning of the war.

Sir Stephen Evans served again as Governor from 1700 to 1712.

Col. John Nicholson, a merchant, was Deputy Governor from 1701 to 1710.

Thomas Lake, a member of the Middle Temple, was Deputy Governor from 1710 to 1711.

Sir Bibye Lake was Governor from 1712-1743, and formerly Deputy Governor from 1711 to 1712. He was a son of Thomas

Lake, and the first Governor to consider the Company his chief interest.

Capt. John Merry was Deputy Governor from 1712 to 1729.

Samuel Jones was Deputy Governor from 1729 to 1735.

The Peace of Utrecht on April 11, 1713, restored all territory belonging to the Company, as defined in the Charter.

Benjamin Pitt was Governor from 1743 to 1746, and was formerly Deputy Governor from 1735 to 1743.

Thomas Knapp was Governor from 1746 to 1750, and was formerly Deputy Governor from 1743 to 1746.

Sir Atwell Lake, son of Sir Bibye Lake, was Governor from 1750 to 1760, and was formerly Deputy Governor from 1746 to 1750.

Sir William Baker was Governor from 1760 to 1770, and was formerly Deputy Governor from 1750 to 1760.

Capt. John Merry was Deputy Governor from 1760 to 1765.

The Treaty of Paris on February 10, 1763, ended the Seven Years War. It resulted in withdrawal of French competition in the fur trade of Rupert's Land.

The Proclamation of July, 1764, ordered free trade with the Indians, subject to the limitations imposed by the Charter. This meant that the exclusive trade in Rupert's Land was lawfully reserved to the Company and was not subject to further legal action.

Sir Bibye Lake was Governor from 1770 to 1782, and formerly Deputy Governor from 1765 to 1770.

Robert Merry was Deputy Governor from 1770 to 1774.

Philip Turnor, the first full-time surveyor, was hired 1778.

"Point" blankets came into use in 1780, on the suggestion of Germain Maugenest.

Samuel Wegg was Governor from 1782 to 1799, and formerly Deputy Governor from 1774 to 1782.

Sir James Winter Lake was Governor from 1799 to 1807, and was formerly Deputy Governor from 1782 to 1799.

Richard Hulse was Deputy Governor from 1799 to 1805.

Nicholas C. Corselis was Deputy Governor from 1805 to 1806.

William Mainwaring was Governor from 1807 to 1812, and was formerly Deputy Governor from 1806 to 1807.

Wedderburn's Retrenching System was promulgated in the Instructions for Trade on May 31, 1810. Each trader was to decide his own standard of trade, to be outfitted by and responsible to the Company; and would receive for wages one-half the profits he made. A tract of land in the Red River area was to be reserved for retired Company servants.

Control of Hudson's Bay Company passed to Thomas Douglas, 5th Earl of Selkirk, by stock purchase early in 1811.

Joseph Berens, Jr. was Governor from 1812 to 1822, and was formerly Deputy Governor from 1807 to 1812.

On June 13, 1811 Lord Selkirk was granted 116,000 square miles between Lake Winnipeg and the headwaters of Red River. The area, officially named Assiniboia, was to be an agricultural colony, distinct from but loosely affiliated with the Company.

The Treaty of Ghent, on December 24, 1814, ended the War of 1812.

The Convention of October 20, 1818 established latitude 49° north as the United States-Canadian boundary from Lake of the Woods to the Rocky Mountains.

An agreement to unite with the North West Company was signed on March 21, 1821. It was approved by the stockholders, on March 26, 1821. The whole trade was to be carried out as one concern, effective June 1, 1821, to run for twenty-one years, in the name of the Hudson's Bay Company. The joint trade was to be conducted by a Board of which the Governor of Hudson's Bay Company was the chairman; with two members from the Hudson's Bay Company (Andrew Wedderburn Colville and Nicholas Garry) and two members from the North West Company (Simon McGillivray and Edward Ellice) completing the Board. The Hudson's Bay Company, as such, with its Charter, Governor and Committee, remained intact. The Committee would nominate its Governor and two members to the Board and would remain outside the scope of the trade agreement.

The Deed Poll also was signed on March 21, 1821. It prescribed that the administration of the fur trade would be conducted by a Governor and Council of Rupert's Land, the Council to be composed of the Chief Factors and the Chief Traders when they were present. The Northern Department was organized to include the Athabaska, Peace, Mackenzie, New Caledonia and Columbia Districts, heretofore outside the chartered limits of Rupert's Land, and claimed by the North West Company by right of exploration, development and occupancy. The Southern Department comprised the area between James Bay and Canada including the eastern shore of Hudson Bay (Ungava).

On July 1, 1821, Nicolas Garry for the Company and Simon McGillivray for the North West Partners arranged the details of the agreement at Fort William. The agreement was ratified by the North West partners on July 11, 1821, in Montreal. Fort William was to be abandoned as a depot, and York Factory was to be the chief depot.

An Act For Regulation of the Fur Trade on July 2, 1821, confirmed the trading monopoly secured by the coalition. The King was given power to grant an exclusive right to the Indian trade in any part of British North America except in Upper and Lower Canada and Rupert's Land. The Crown thus got no right to override the chartered rights of the Company within its own territory.

A Royal Proclamation dated December 5, 1821, granted a Royal License for Exclusive Trade in all parts of British North America except in the two provinces of Canada and in Rupert's Land (exclusive trade in Rupert's Land was granted in the Charter) to the Governor and Committee of the Hudson's Bay Company and to William and Simon McGillivray and to Edward Ellice as agents for the North West Company, to run for 21 years. It did not exclude Americans from trading in the Oregon country, which was under Joint Occupation according to the Convention of 1818. The joint companies were responsible for the administration of justice throughout their trading domain.

The same day, December 5, 1821, the Company and the former North West agents entered into a Deed of Covenant to keep the terms of the grant.

On May 29, 1822, by a Resolution of the General Court of

the Company, either of the two Governors and their Councils of Rupert's Land took precedence over the Governor and Council of Assiniboia when they were in the colony; when they were actually present for judicial purposes, the Governor of Assiniboia was to be suspended.

Sir John H. Pelly, Baronet, was Governor from 1822 to 1852, and was formerly Deputy Governor from 1812 to 1822.

Nicolas Garry was Deputy Governor from 1822 to 1835.

Benjamin Harrison was Deputy Governor from 1835 to 1839.

William and Simon McGillivray and Edward Ellice surrendered their individual interests to Hudson's Bay Company on August 25, 1824, and received stock in the Company, thus becoming ordinary share-holders. The joint committee, on which they were entitled to two places, was dissolved September 15, 1824 and unity of control by the Governor and Committee was completely achieved.

The License for Exclusive Trade was extended on May 13, 1838, to expire on May 30, 1859. It omitted the names of William and Simon McGillivray and Edward Ellice who had become ordinary shareholders. The License was qualified by making it subject to possible creation of colonies.

The Oregon Boundary Treaty on June 15, 1846, set the boundary at latitude 49° north from the crest of the Rocky Mountains to the Pacific Ocean. Great Britain got all of Vancouver Island. The Company's rights were defined by Secretary of State William L. Marcy (1853-1857) as rights to the land but not the right to trade in American territory. The possessory rights were satisfied in September, 1869, by a joint United States-Hudson's Bay Company commission which awarded the Company $650,000 paid in gold in 1870 and 1871.

Andrew (Wedderburn) Colville was Governor from 1852 to 1856, and was formerly Deputy Governor from 1839 to 1852. He was a brother-in-law of Lord Selkirk and was the originator of Wedderburn's Retrenching System of 1810.

John Shepherd was Governor from 1856 to 1858, and was formerly Deputy Governor from 1852 to 1856.

Henry H. Behrens was Governor from 1858 to 1863, and was formerly Deputy Governor from 1856 to 1858.

Edward Ellice was Deputy Governor from 1858 to 1863.

On June 15, 1863, the entire interests of Hudson's Bay Company were sold to the International Financial Society, Robert Benson, president, a syndicate of bankers organized on May 11, 1863. The transaction was handled by Richard Potter for the syndicate and Henry Behrens, Governor of the Company. Shares were to be taken up as presented at £300 for each £100 share until the Society acquired control, which occurred early in July, 1863. This marked the end of the regime for which fur-trading was the chief consideration. The last meeting of the old Committee was held June 30, 1863.

Sir Edmund W. Head, former Governor-General of Canada, was elected Governor on July 2, 1863, at the first meeting of the new Committee. He died in office on January 29, 1868.

Sir Curtis M. Lampson was Deputy Governor from 1863 to 1870.

Earl of Kimberly was Governor from 1868 to 1869.

The Rupert's Land Act passed by Parliament July 31, 1868; officially called "An Act for Enabling Her Majesty to Accept a Surrender upon Terms of the Lands, Privileges and Rights of 'The Governor and Company of Adventurers of England Trading into Hudson's Bay' and for Admitting the Same into the Dominion of Canada." The Crown was enabled, by Order-in-Council, to declare Rupert's Land a part of the Dominion of Canada; and the parliament of Canada was given authority to govern over the land. Until the whole operation should be completed, and Rupert's Land had been brought within the Dominion, the existing authorities (i.e., the Company) were to remain responsible for government and administration.

Sir Stafford Northcote, Earl of Iddelsleight, was Governor from 1869 to 1874.

Eden Colville was Deputy Governor from 1871 to 1880.

The terms of the settlement, negotiated by Sir Georges Cartier and William McDougall for Canada, were: Canada would pay

84

Ł 300, 000 for the territory of Rupert's Land except a portion reserved by the Company which was 1/20 of the fertile belt bounded
on the south by the United States, on the west by the Rocky Mountains, on the east by Lake Winnipeg, Lake of the Woods and the
waters connecting them. In addition, the Company would retain
45, 000 acres adjacent to each trading post.

The Governor and Committee accepted the terms of the
settlement on March 20, 1869, the General Court of shareholders
accepted it on April 9, 1869, and the Canadian Parliament accepted
it on June 1, 1869.

On June 22, 1869, in anticipation of formal transfer, the
Canadian Parliament passed an Act for the Temporary Government
of Rupert's Land and the North West Territory when United with
Canada. The name North West Territories was given to the entire
area, and provision was made for the appointment of a Lieutenant-
Governor to administer justice and establish laws, subject to their
ratification by the Parliament.

William McDougall was appointed Lieutenant-Governor on
September 28, 1869.

The Corporate Seal of the Company was affixed to the Deed
of Surrender by Governor Northcote, November 19, 1869, with
December 1, 1869 fixed as the date for transfer.

The Riel Rebellion of 1869 delayed the formal transfer.
(See under Assiniboia). Company rule theoretically ended on
December 1, 1869, and the Colonial Office was theoretically in
control, but a provisional government headed by Louis Riel was in
actual control.

The Deed of Surrender was sent to the Colonial Office on
May 7, 1870. The Company received the Ł 300, 000 on May 10, 1870.

Imperial Order-in-Council, on June 23, 1870, formally
completed the transfer and admission into the Dominion. Effective
July 15, 1870, the governmental functions of the Hudson's Bay
Company were ended.

Governors in Rupert's Land

The Charter provided that a Governor and Council be appointed to act in the territory for the Governor and Committee in London.

Charles Bayly was Governor from 1670 to 1674. He was appointed "Bay" Governor before the Charter was signed. With Radisson, and Groseilliers, he arrived at Fort Charles on September 8, 1670 and made it his first headquarters.

Father Charles Albanel, a Jesuit, claimed Fort Charles for France on June 28, 1672, during Bayly's absence, and Bayly built a post on Hayes Island in the Moose River in 1673.

William Lydall was Governor from 1674 to 1675. He arrived on September 18, 1674, spent the winter only, and returned to England in the spring, 1675.

Charles Bayly had remained on the Bay, and he resumed the Governorship when Lydall left. He served as Governor from 1675 to 1679. His chief post after Lydall's departure was Moose.

Bayly built Albany post on Bayly Island in the Chichewan (Albany) River in 1679 and put John Bridgar in charge (1679-1681). Charles Bayly died in London on January 6, 1680.

John Nixon was Governor from 1679 to 1683. He built a warehouse on Charleston Island for the transfer of goods from ocean vessels to Bay vessels in 1680-1681.

On May 15, 1682, John Bridgar was named Governor of a fort to be erected in the Hayes-Nelson area, which was to be independent of the Governor at the Bottom of the Bay.

Governors at the Bottom of the Bay 1683-1714

Henry Sergeant was appointed Governor on January 31, 1683. In 1684, he made Albany his headquarters.

Pierre, Chevalier de Troyes, supported by the Compagnie du Nord (Compagnie de la Baie d'Hudson), a French trading company chartered by Charles Aubert, Sieur de la Chesney in Quebec, in March 1684, left Montreal overland to Hudson Bay in March, 1686.

On June 21, 1686, he captured Moose Factory from Anthony Dowage, temporarily in charge, and renamed it Fort Saint Louis. On July 3, 1686, he captured Fort Charles from Hugh Verner in charge, along with Deputy Governor John Bridgar, and renamed it

Fort Saint Jacques. On July 26, 1686, he captured Fort Albany, (and Governor Sergeant), and renamed it Fort Sainte Anne. De Troyes left for Quebec in October 1686, leaving Pierre le Moyne, Sieur d'Iberville, in charge. D'Iberville was confirmed in his command by Denonville, Governor of New France.

Captain John Marsh was Governor in 1688. He was sent to rebuild Albany post. He changed the site from Bayly's Island, at that time occupied by Fort Sainte Anne under d'Iberville, to Churchill Island nearby. Governor Marsh died late in December, 1688.

Captain Andrew Hamilton was Governor from 1688 to 1689. On March 10, 1689, he surrendered to the French under d'Iberville, who then occupied the post on Churchill Island. D'Iberville left for Quebec in September, 1689, leaving a small party at Albany post.

James Knight, who was Governor from 1693 to 1700, recaptured Albany post on July 2, 1693, from six Frenchmen remaining there. In 1693, the French posts at Moose and Rupert were destroyed by the French to prevent their capture by the British.

The Treaty of Ryswick, signed on September 20, 1697, restored possessions of each side as they had been at the beginning of the war. Actually, neither side observed these terms as applied to conditions in Hudson's Bay.

John Fullartine was Governor from 1700 to 1705.

Anthony Beale was Governor from 1705 to 1708. His commission was dated September 13, 1705.

John Fullartine was Governor again from 1708 to 1711. His commission was dated May 26, 1708.

Anthony Beale was Governor again from 1711 to 1714. His commission was dated May 27, 1711, and he arrived on September 26, 1711.

James Knight was appointed Governor of the Bay on May 20, 1713, after the Peace of Utrecht, to accept return of the posts then held by the French to the Hudson's Bay Company. He made his headquarters at York Fort. Albany, nominally under the control of Knight, was, in fact, virtually independent.

Governors at York Fort 1682-1713

On May 15, 1682, John Bridgar was named Governor of a post to be erected on the Hayes or Nelson River, to be independent of Governor Nixon at Albany.

New Englanders under Ben Gillam arrived on the Nelson River on August 19, 1682, and built a house on Bachelor's Island, 26 miles upstream from the mouth, on the north bank of the Nelson River.

Radisson and Groseilliers, now working for the Compagnie de la Baie d'Hudson, chartered by Charles Aubert, Sieur de la Chesnay of Quebec in 1682, arrived on the Hayes River, on August 20, 1682. They built a house on Rainbow Island, on the south bank of the Hayes River, ten miles upstream from the mouth, and named it Fort Bourbon.

John Bridgar and Zechariah Gillam arrived on the Nelson River on August 26, 1682. Bridgar built a house on the south bank of the Hayes River on September 18, 1682. Gillam and the Company ship, the Rupert, were lost on October 21, 1682.

Radisson captured Gillam's party in February, 1683, and burned their house. He captured Bridgar's party on June 6, 1683 and destroyed their house. He took the prisoners to Quebec on October 20, 1685. All were released by Governor de la Barre. Jean Baptiste Chouart, son of Groseilliers, was left at Fort Bourbon to trade with the Indians.

John Abraham was Governor from 1683 to 1685. He arrived after Radisson had left with his prisoners, and built Port Nelson on the north shore of the Nelson River in 1683.

Radisson, again working for the Hudson's Bay Company, arrived on August 11, 1684. He removed Chouart and abandoned Fort Bourbon, leaving the Company in possession of the Hayes-Nelson area.

Governor Abraham and Radisson built Hayes Fort on the south bank of the Nelson River in 1684 and York Fort, on the north bank of the Hayes River. George Geyer was put in charge of York
88

Fort.

Sieur de la Martinière, working for the Compagnie du Nord, arrived on September 22, 1684 (N.S.) and built a post on the south bank of Hayes River. He wintered there, and then left for Quebec on July 15, 1685.

Thomas Phipps was Governor from 1685 to 1688. The New Severn post was built in 1685, on the New Severn River, by George Geyer. It was named Ft. Churchill, and Samuel Missenden was put in charge from 1685 to 1687.

Churchill River post was built in 1688, and Thomas Savage put in charge from 1687 to 1690.

George Geyer was Governor from 1688 to 1693. He was Governor and chief over the Hayes-Nelson area and the posts at Churchill River and New Severn River, and the headquarters at York Fort. He was given a Royal Commission to make treaties with the Indians and to seize French ships.

Henry Kelsey, explored the edge of the Barren Grounds from Churchill River post in the summer of 1689, but returned to York Fort when the post accidentally burned during his absence.

Thomas Walsh, chief of Ft. Churchill on the New Severn River, from 1687 to 1690, burned this post in 1690, to prevent its capture by d'Iberville, He went overland to York Fort.

Henry Kelsey left York Fort on June 12, 1690 in company with the Stone Indians (Assiniboines). He named Dering's Point (possibly the Pas, Manitoba) on July 10, 1690, and explored to the Great Plains west of Lake Winnipegosis in 1690-1691 returning to York Fort in 1692.

Thomas Walsh was Governor from 1693 to 1694.

Pierre le Moyne, Sieur d'Iberville was Governor from 1694 to 1695. On October 15, 1694, he captured York Fort from Governor Walsh, renamed it Fort Bourbon. The English were turned into the woods for the winter, and were taken prisoner to Quebec when d'Iberville departed on September 7, 1695.

Gabriel, Sieur de la Forest was Governor from 1695 to 1696.

Captain William Allen recaptured York Fort on August 28,

1696 and sent de la Forest to England. Captain Allen left for England, and was killed in a naval battle off the Scilly Islands.

Captain Henry Baley was Governor from 1696 to 1697. He had been Deputy Governor under Captain Allen. Henry Kelsey was his Deputy Governor.

Pierre le Moyne, Sieur d'Iberville captured York Fort again on September 3, 1697, and renamed it Fort Bourbon. He returned to France by November, 1697.

Joseph le Moyne, Sieur de Serigny, a brother of d'Iberville, was Governor from 1697 to 1698.

Jean Baptiste le Moyne, Sieur de Montigny, a cousin of d'Iberville and Serigny, was Governor from 1698 to 1708.

Nicolas Jérémie was Governor from 1708 to 1714. He turned Fort Bourbon over to the English under James Knight, as required by the Peace of Utrecht, September 11, 1713.

James Knight was Governor of the Bay from 1714 to 1718. His headquarters were at York Fort. William Stewart, sent to explore from York Fort, reached the country southeast of Great Slave Lake in 1716.

Churchill River post was re-established by Knight in 1717 with Richard Staunton first chief from 1717 to 1721. It was named Prince of Wales Fort on August 17, 1719.

Henry Kelsey was Governor of the Bay from 1718 to 1722. His commission was dated May 30, 1718.

James Knight was lost on a voyage of discovery in 1719, when his ship was wrecked on Marble Island.

Thomas McLeish was Governor from 1722 to 1734. He was named Governor of the Bay in 1727.

Albany post was moved back to Bayly's Island in 1721-1722. It was fortified, and named Fort Albany.

A post was built on Eastmain River in 1723-1724. It was dependent on Albany and was not permanently staffed. A sloop captain commanded the fort.

Moose post was rebuilt in 1730 to 1731. Thomas Render, sloop-master, was its first commander in 1731. William Bevan, sloop-master from Eastmain, was appointed chief in the fall of 1731.

First stone fort in the Arctic was built at Fort Prince of Wales. It was begun in 1731, and was made independent of York Fort, with Richard Norton as chief from 1731 to 1741.

Thomas White was Governor from 1734 to 1737.

James Isham was Governor from 1737 to 1748. He was appointed on May 4, 1737. He lived at Fort Prince of Wales from 1741 to 1746, arriving there on August 16, 1741. Thomas White was chief at York Fort from 1741 to 1746.

Henley House was built in 1743 by Joseph Isbister as an outpost of Fort Albany. William Isbister was its first master from 1743 to 1751. All personnel, including Master William Lamb (1751-1755) were killed by Indians in January 1755. The post was rebuilt by September 1, 1759 by George Clark, who was appointed master. He was killed on September 17, 1759 by French and Indians. The post lapsed until 1768 when it was rebuilt.

Capt. John Newton was Governor from 1748 to 1758.

Anthony Henday left York Fort June 26, 1754, in company of Cree Indians. He reached Moose Lake on the lower Saskatchewan River on July 16, 1754. The westernmost point reached on November 21, 1754, was near the present site of Calgary. He returned to York Fort on June 20, 1755.

Humphrey Marten was Governor from 1758 to 1762.

Chesterfield Inlet was discovered in 1760, by Captain William Christopher in the sloop Churchill, sailing from Fort Prince of Wales.

Ferdinand Jacobs was Governor from 1762 to 1775. He was on leave 1765-1766 and 1771-1772, with Andrew Graham Acting Governor during both intervals.

Samuel Hearne, in company of Matonabbee and Chipewyan Indians, left Fort Prince of Wales on December 7, 1770. They reached mouth of Coppermine River and started back on July 18, 1771, finished crossing the Great Slave Lake (the first white man to see this lake) on January 9, 1772 and returning to Fort Prince of Wales on June 30, 1772.

Samuel Hearne, working from York Fort, built a post at Cumberland House on Cumberland Lake in 1774. He returned to

York Fort in June, 1775, leaving John Garrioch in charge. Hearne was appointed chief by Governor Jacobs, but orders from London made Hearne Chief at Fort Prince of Wales and Matthew Cocking chief of Cumberland (1775-1777).

Humphrey Marten was Governor from 1775 to 1786. He was on leave from 1781 to 1782, leaving Matthew Cocking as Acting Governor.

Fort Prince of Wales, Samuel Hearne, chief from 1775 to 1787 surrendered to the French under Comte Jean-François la Pérouse on August 8, 1782. York Fort, under Governor Marten, surrendered on August 24, 1782. Both forts were destroyed; Hearne and Marten were taken to Cadiz when la Pérouse departed on September 1, 1782. Both were released, and were re-appointed to their posts. York and Churchill posts were rebuilt, but the stone fort at Fort Prince of Wales was abandoned.

William Tomison served as Inland Chief at York from 1786 to 1804. York was to be the factory for the supply of inland posts, the Chief was to reside inland, exercise maximum mobility. He had full powers to allocate men and supplies to the inland posts. Joseph Colen was appointed Resident Chief at York, from 1786 to 1798, to preside during Tomison's absence, but to yield to him when the Chief came to the factory.

Tomison was on leave from 1795 to 1796, with George Sutherland Acting.

Edward Jarvis was Supervisor and Inspector over all Hudson's Bay Posts from 1795 to 1798.

Tomison was Chief without limitation at York, from 1798 to 1804. He retired in 1804, and was permitted to become an independent trader, backed by the Company, and receiving a commission on all trade he obtained.

Re-organization 1810-1815

In February, 1810, Rupert's Land was divided into a Northern and a Southern Department, as part of Wedderburn's Retrenching System.

The Northern Department based on York Territory consisted

of York, Churchill, Winnipeg and Saskatchewan districts. The Winnipeg district was divided into East Winnipeg and West Winnipeg in 1811. The Superintendent of the Northern Department was William Auld from 1810 to 1814. He was appointed on May 30, 1810 and resigned September 15, 1813; the resignation was accepted April 9, 1814.

The Southern Department based on Moose Factory, consisted of Moose, Albany and Eastmain districts. Superintendent of the Southern Department from 1810 to 1814 was Thomas Thomas.

Re-organization of 1814

The Northern Department was divided into the districts of York Factory Saskatchewan Inland, with its chief at Edmonton; Churchill Inland, with its chief at Deer's Lake; West Winnipeg, with its chief at Cumberland; East Winnipeg, with its chief at Norway House, and the Rocky Mountain district.

Thomas Thomas was Superintendent from 1814 to 1815. He retired in 1815.

The Southern Department divided into the districts of Moose Factory and Albany. Thomas Vincent was Superintendent from 1814 to 1816. He was appointed Chief Factor by the Deed Poll of March 21, 1821, and retired effective June 1, 1826.

Governors-in-Chief   1815-1870

Robert Semple was Governor-in-Chief from 1815 to 1816. He was put over the Superintendents of the Northern and the Southern Departments and over the Governor of Assiniboia as well.

Athabaska District was created in 1816 to compete against the North West Company. Colin Robertson was in charge from 1816 to 1820.

Governor Semple was killed at Seven Oaks on June 19, 1816, and James Bird was temporary Governor-in-Chief from 1816 to 1818.

William Williams was appointed Governor-in-Chief in May 1818 and served until 1821.

The Convention of October 20, 1818 established the United States-Canadian boundary at latitude 49° north from Lake of the Woods to the crest of the Rocky Mountains.

George Simpson was appointed Associate Governor-in-Chief on February 26, 1820, to act in case Williams was out of the country. He was put in charge of the Athabaska District, with his command post at Fort Wedderburn.

Hudson's Bay Company merged with the North West Company on March 21, 1821. William Williams was appointed Governor of the Northern Department on March 28, 1821, to be the senior executive officer of the combined Hudson Bay Company-North West Company coaliation. He was based at York Factory. George Simpson was appointed Governor of the Southern Department on March 29, 1821. He was based at Moose Factory.

George Simpson was Governor from 1821 to 1860.

The appointment of William Williams as chief executive was not agreeable to the North West partners, so Nicolas Garry, at York, made George Simpson Governor of the Northern Department, hence chief executive, and William Williams was made Governor of the Southern Department in October, 1821. This was confirmed by the Governor and Committee on February 27, 1822.

By a Resolution of the General Court of the Company on May 29, 1822, either of the two Governors and their councils took precedence over the Governor and Council of Assiniboia when they were in the colony.

William Williams, Governor of the Southern Department was recalled on February 26, 1826, and George Simpson was given authority over both Departments. His official appointment was made in December, 1826. Theoretically the two departments remained separate until 1839 when Simpson was made Governor-in-Chief.

Eden Colville was appointed Associate Governor of Rupert's Land and Acting Governor of Assiniboia. He presided in Council from September 5, 1850 to May 1, 1851.

Governor Simpson died in office on September 7, 1860.

Alexander Grant Dallas was Governor from 1860 to 1864.

William MacTavish was appointed Governor on January 28, 1869 and served until 1870.

Rupert's Land ceased to exist as a territorial entity on July 15, 1870 when the land was transferred to Canada. MacTavish was the last Company Governor of Assiniboia as well.

ASSINIBOIA-MANITOBA

Property of the Selkirks 1811-1836

Thomas Douglas, Baron Daer, 5th Lord Selkirk, was granted 116,000 square miles between Lake Winnipeg and the headquarters
of the Red River on June 12, 1811. This colony, which was devoted
to agriculture, was distinctly different from the fur-trading function
of the Hudson's Bay Company. The colony was officially named
Assiniboia, popularly called the Red River Colony. The Governor
was appointed by Selkirk or his heirs, and given a commission in
the Hudson's Bay Company.

Captain Miles Macdonell was the first Governor, serving
from 1811 to 1816. Governor Macdonell and the first settlers arrived at the fork of the Assiniboia and Red Rivers on August 30,
1812, and took formal possession September 4, 1812. He established Fort Douglas, near the North West Company post of Fort Gibraltar, under the command of Alexander Macdonell. Fort Daer, at
the junction of the Red and Pembina Rivers was built as a buffalo
hunting station.

Under the Treaty of Ghent on December 24, 1814, the boundary west from Lake of the Woods was to remain unsurveyed beyond
the point at which it intersected latitude $49°$ north.

Duncan Cameron, a North West partner, arrested Miles
Macdonell on June 16, 1815, and sent him to Montreal for trial.
Cameron also persuaded most of the colonists to desert to Jack
River on Lake Winnipeg. The Métis, under Cuthbert Grant, terror-
ized the remaining settlers, who fled to Mossy Point on Lake Winni-
peg. George Campbell, North Wester, destroyed Fort Douglas.

Colin Robertson was recruiting officer for the colony and
the Company. He left Montreal, in May, 1815, for the colony.
He met Miles Macdonell, then under arrest, on the way to Montreal,
who gave him the news about desertion of the settlers. Robertson
went to Jack River, rallied the colonists and led them back to Fort
Douglas, which was rebuilt in September, 1815.

Robert Semple, Governor-in-Chief of Rupert's Land from 1815 to 1816, arrived at Fort Douglas on November 3, 1815, and left on an inspection tour, leaving Robertson in charge of the colony for the winter of 1815-1816. During this time, Robertson occupied Fort Gibraltar, and arrested Duncan Cameron in March, 1816, sending him to York Fort. Governor Semple came to reside in the colony in the spring of 1816. Robertson left for York Fort on June 11, 1816. Governor Semple was killed by Métis under Cuthbert Grant, at the Massacre of Seven Oaks, near Fort Douglas on June 19, 1816, after Semple had destroyed Fort Gibraltar.

Lord Selkirk arrived in Canada in the autumn of 1815, and learned by note from Robertson of the dispersal of the colonists. He hired the deMeuron Regiment of Swiss and German Protestants (140 men) the Watteville Regiment of Foreigners (40 men) and a small part of Glengarry Fencibles. He secured the release of Macdonell, and started for the colony on June 16, 1816, sending Macdonell on ahead.

Macdonell arrived back at the colony, discovered the massacre and turned back toward Montreal, meeting Selkirk at Sault Ste. Marie.

Selkirk captured Fort William on August 13, 1816, arrested William McGillivray and other North West partners, and sent them to Montreal for trial. He remained in possession of Fort William. He sent Macdonell and the deMeuron Regiment to recapture Fort Daer and Fort Douglas from the Métis. This mission was accomplished by January 10, 1817 when Fort Douglas was retaken.

McGillivray, free on bail in Montreal, obtained a warrant for the arrest of Selkirk. Selkirk refused arrest when this warrant was presented at Fort William in November, 1816.

A Commission of Enquiry was appointed to mediate between the two parties. Colonel W.B. Coltman and Major J. Fletcher were appointed Commissioners on October 30, 1816, to arrest all perpetrators, sending them to Montreal for trial. They were unable to reach Fort William before winter.

Selkirk went on to Fort Douglas and arrived there on June 21, 1817. Commissioner Coltman followed. He presented to Selkirk the Prince Regent's Proclamation of May 1, 1817, put out by the Acting Governor of Lower Canada, Sir Gordon Drummond, requiring both sides to restore all goods seized during the conflict. Selkirk complied, the North Westers reneged. Selkirk accepted the warrant for his arrest, was freed on bail, the North Westers fled to avoid arrest.

Selkirk completed his work for the colony, and set up a Governor (Alexander Macdonell) and Council, as well as a court of law. He left the colony September 9, 1817, and reached Montreal shortly thereafter. He was freed of the charges against him while the North Westers escaped through various legal manipulations. Selkirk left Canada in November, 1818, and retired to France where he died on April 8, 1820. Assiniboia remained in the Selkirk family, and continued to be administered by a Governor and Council, separate from the Hudson's Bay Company establishment.

Alexander Macdonell had taken charge of the colony after the death of Governor Semple on June 19, 1816. He was appointed Governor by Selkirk in August, 1817, and served until 1822.

Andrew Bulger was Governor from June, 1822 to July, 1823. Governor Simpson, Governor of the Northern Department of Rupert's Land, governed personally between governors.

Robert P. Pelly was Governor from July, 1823 to June 1825. He was a cousin of the Governor of Hudson's Bay Company, Sir John H. Pelly.

Donald McKenzie was Governor from June, 1825 to June, 1833. He was also Chief Factor for Hudson's Bay Company.

Lower Fort Garry was built in 1831-1832, 20 miles downstream from the fork of the Red and Assiniboine Rivers.

Alexander Christie was Governor from June, 1833 to June 13, 1839. He was also Chief Factor for Hudson's Bay Company.

Upper Fort Garry was built in 1835, at the fork of the Red and Assiniboia Rivers, now the City of Winnipeg.

Property of Hudson's Bay Company 1836-1870

Hudson's Bay Company bought back the colony from the 6th Earl of Selkirk for £ 15,000 of Company stock, the date of the reconveyance was May 4, 1836. The Governor and Council were now to be appointed by the Company.

The First Legislative Council met on February 12, 1835. It was dominated by Company men.

Duncan Finlayson was Governor from June 13, 1839 to June, 1844. He was also Chief Factor for Hudson's Bay Company.

Alexander Christie was Governor again from June 19, 1844 to September 20, 1848.

Col. John Crofton, of the 6th Regiment of Foot was Acting Governor from June, 1846 to June, 1847.

Major John T. Griffiths, of the 6th Regiment of Foot, was Acting Governor from June, 1847 to September 20, 1848.

Major William Bletterman Caldwell was appointed Governor on June 10, 1848, and took office September 20, 1848. His term ended on February 27, 1856. He was an Officer in the 92nd Regiment of Foot.

Francis G. Johnson was appointed Deputy Governor to act in the absence of Governor Caldwell on June 28, 1855, and was appointed Governor on November 28, 1855. He took office on February 27, 1856 and served until 1858.

William MacTavish was inaugurated as Governor on December 9, 1858. He was the last governor of Assiniboia. He was also the last Governor of Rupert's Land. (See p. 94)

The Red River Rebellion of 1869-1870

On September 28, 1869, William McDougall was appointed Governor by John Alexander Macdonald, Prime Minister of Canada.

The actual beginning of the rebellion came on October 11, 1869. A survey party under Major Webb was forcibly stopped at St. Vital by André Mault.

On October 20, 1869, a Comité National des Métis de la Rivière Rouge was formed, with John Bruce as president and Louis-David Riel as secretary.

Governor-designate, William McDougall, was forbidden to enter the colony at Pembina, Minnesota, on October 30, 1869.

Riel occupied Fort Garry on November 2, 1869.

On November 22, 1869, a provisional government was

organized and agreement was made among the rebels to continue under the Governor and Council of the Hudson's Bay Company. An executive council was elected to treat with the Canadian government.

On November 26, 1869, Prime Minister John Alexander Macdonald, learning of the trouble, wired the Canadian representative in London, John Rose, not to pay over the purchase money until McDougall could secure peaceable possession of the colony.

During the night of November 30, 1869, Governor-designate William McDougall slipped across the boundary from Pembina, into the colony, and read two spurious proclamations, after which he withdrew to American territory. The first proclamation declared that from and after December 1, 1869, Rupert's Land and the North West Territories were part of the Dominion of Canada and McDougall was the Lieutenant-Governor by virtue of his commission of September 28, 1869 from the Governor-General of Canada. The second proclamation announced McDougall's entry upon office and called upon all officers of the colony, except Governor McTavish, to continue their public duties. On the basis of these proclamations Governor McTavish considered that his duties as Governor were over.

On December 8, 1869, Riel, insisting that a provisional government must rule between the time the Company laid down the authority on December 1, 1869, and the constitution of full Provincial government within the Dominion, proclaimed a Provisional Government, to date from November 24, 1869. This body became known as the First Provisional Government.

On December 10, 1869, Donald A. Smith, Chief of the Montreal District of Hudson's Bay Company, was appointed by Prime Minister Macdonald as a Special Commissioner to deal with the rebels and secure a peaceful transfer to Canada. He had in hand the genuine Royal Proclamation of December 6, 1869.

Governor-designate McDougall returned to Canada on December 18, 1869.

John Bruce resigned as Provisional president on December 27, 1869, the office taken by Riel.

February 10, 1870. A Second Provisional Government was

organized, this time including English settlers and continuing Riel as president. Alfred Scott, Reverend N. J. Richtot and Judge John Black were elected commissioners to deal with Canada over terms for entering the Dominion. Riel wanted full Provincial status, the Ministry wanted to give the colony territorial status.

On May 2, 1870, a bill was introduced, constituting the old district of Assiniboia into a new Province of Manitoba. The Act of June 22, 1869 was re-enacted temporarily for the new and limited North West Territories; it provided that the Lieutenant-Governor of Manitoba should also be the Lieutenant-Governor of the North West Territories.

On May 3, 1870, orders were issued for paying over the purchase money to the Hudson's Bay Company.

Sir Adam G. Archibald was appointed first Lieutenant-Governor of Manitoba and the North West Territories on May 20, 1870.

By Imperial Order-in-Council, issued on June 23, 1870, and effective on July 15, 1870, Rupert's Land, formerly under Charter to the Hudson's Bay Company, and the old North West Territory, would be transferred to the Dominion of Canada.

Assiniboia, as the Province of Manitoba, came into the Dominion of Canada as the 5th Province on July 15, 1870.

Riel went into exile in the United States when Colonel Garnet Wolseley and troops sent by the Colonial Office (London) arrived in Red River August 22, 1870, to publish the Proclamation.

Lieutenant-Governors 1870-

Sir Adam G. Archibald. Commissioned May 20, 1870.

Francis G. Johnson. Commissioned April 9, 1872.

Alexander Morris. Commissioned December 2, 1872.

Joseph E. Cauchon. Commissioned October 8, 1877.

James C. Aikins. Commissioned September 29, 1882.

J. C. Schulz. Commissioned July 1, 1888.

J. C. Patterson. Commissioned September 2, 1895.

Sir Daniel H. McMillan. Commissioned October 10, 1900.

Sir Douglas C. Cameron. Commissioned August 1, 1911.

Sir James A. M. Aikins. Commissioned August 3, 1916.

Theodore A. Burrows. Commissioned October 9, 1926.

J. D. McGregor. Commissioned January 25, 1929.

William J. Tupper. Commissioned December 1, 1934.

Roland F. McWilliams. Commissioned November 1, 1940.

John S. McDiarmid. Commissioned August 1, 1953.

Errick F. Willis. Commissioned January 15, 1960.

Richard S. Bowes. Commissioned September 1, 1965.

Premiers 1870-

A. Boyd. Conservative. Appointed September 16, 1870.

N. A. Girard. Conservative. Appointed December 14, 1871.

J. H. Clarke. Conservative. Appointed March 14, 1872.

N. A. Girard. Conservative. Appointed July 8, 1874.

R. A. Davis. Conservative. Appointed December 3, 1874.

John Norquay. Conservative. Appointed October 16, 1878.

D. H. Harrison. Conservative. Appointed December 26, 1887.

T. Greenway. Liberal. Appointed January 19, 1888.

H. J. Macdonald. Conservative. Appointed January 8, 1900.

Sir R. P. Robin. Conservative. Appointed October 29, 1900.

T. C. Norris. Conservative. Appointed May 12, 1915.

John Bracken. Coalition. Appointed August 8, 1922.

S. S. Garson. Coalition. Appointed January 8, 1943.

D. L. Campbell. Liberal. Appointed November 7, 1948.

Dufferin Roblin. Conservative. Appointed June 16, 1958.

Walter Weir. Appointed November 27, 1967.

THE NORTH WEST COMPANY

French Fur-Traders 1658-1689

In 1658, a lease of exclusive privileges was granted by
the king in an agreement known as the Traite (trade) de Tadoussac.
By this agreement, trade which had formerly been carried out as
a business venture of the king, was turned over to one Sieur De-
maure, who would bear the expenses for a share of the profits.
The Domaine du Roi, originally roughly the area that had belonged
to the Saguenay Indians was modified to include the territory from
the Ile aux Coudres to the Baie des Sept Iles along the northern
shore of the St. Lawrence River, and extending north to the headwaters of the streams draining into the St. Lawrence. Trading
posts in this area were known as the Postes du Roi.

The lease passed to the Compagnie des Postes du Roi in
1700, and was renewed every 21 years. After the conquest, the
British Government adopted the practice of leasing to the highest
bidder; in 1765 the lease went to Dunn and Company. The North
West Company acquired the lease in 1788, and passed it on to the
Hudson's Bay Company after the merger of 1821. The lease was
renewed in 1842 and expired by limitation in 1859.

Daniel Greysolon DuLhut (Duluth), in the summer of 1679,
built a fur-trading post at Kaministikwia on Lake Superior, on the
site of the future Fort William, headquarters for the North West
Company. The post lasted until about 1700.

In 1684, with his brother Charles Greysolon DuLhut, he
built a post on the shore of Lake Nipigon near the á la Manne River.

Jacques de Noyon reached Rainy Lake, and wintered there
in 1688-89.

The Postes du Nord   1717-1759

Beginning in 1717, a series of posts were to be erected,
primarily as bases for exploration westward from Lake Superior and

secondarily as fur-trading posts. King Louis XV had refused financial assistance, and all expenses of exploration were to be met from proceeds of the fur trade. The posts came to be known as the Postes du Nord, and the Commander was selected by the Governor of New France.

Zacharie Robutel de la Nöue was Commander from 1717 to 1721. In 1717, he erected a new fort at Kaministikwia, which became the staging area for exploration.

Jean Baptiste Deschaillons de Saint-Ours was Commander from 1721 to 1729.

Pierre Gaultier de Varennes, Sieur de la Vérendrye, was Commander from 1729 to 1744. He resigned in 1744.

In 1731, he sent his nephew, Christophe du Frost, Sieur de la Jemeray, from Kaministikwia, to build Fort Saint Pierre, two miles west of present Fort Frances, on Rainy Lake.

In 1732, he built Fort Saint Charles (on present American Point in the Northwest Angle) on Lake of the Woods. This fort became his headquarters.

In 1734, he sent René Cartier to build Fort Maurepas (near present Selkirk, Manitoba) on the Red River. It was abandoned in 1742.

Fort la Reine (near present Portage La Prairie, Manitoba), was built in 1738. Vérendrye left from here on October 16, 1738 and reached a Mantanna Indian village (near present Sanish, North Dakota) on December 3, 1738. He left on December 13, 1738 and reached Fort la Reine on February 10, 1739.

His sons, Louis-Joseph, Chevalier de la Vérendrye, and François, Sieur de Tremblay, left Fort la Reine on April 29, 1742, to explore the Great Plains. Louis-Joseph, with a band of Bow Indians, reached farthest west in vicinity of Big Horn Mountains, Wyoming on January 12, 1743. He buried a lead plate at the junction of the Bad and Missouri Rivers (Pierre, South Dakota) on March 30, 1743. Both sons reached Fort la Reine on July 2, 1743.

Nicolas-Joseph de Noyelles, Sieur de Fleurimont, was Commander from 1744 to 1746. He was a nephew by marriage of LaVérendrye. He resigned in 1746.

Pierre Gaultier de Varennes, Sieur de LaVérendrye, resumed

the post of Commander from 1746 to 1749. He died on December 5, 1749, in Montreal.

Son Louis-Joseph, Chevalier de la Vérendrye, reached the forks of the Saskatchewan River in 1749.

Captain Jacques Repentigny Legardeur de Saint-Pierre was Commander from 1750 to 1753. He made his headquarters at Fort la Reine.

Louis Chapt, Chevalier de la Corne, was Commander from 1753 to 1755. He built Fort la Corne below the forks of the Saskatchewan (Fort Saint Louis des Prairies), in 1753. This post completed a chain of forts which controlled the headwaters of the rivers flowing into Hudson Bay and thus intercepting the Indians on their way to Bay posts to trade. The French abandoned these posts after the beginning of the French and Indian War which ran from 1759 to 1763.

The Montreal Traders 1761-1784

Even before the Treaty of Paris in 1763, English and French fur-traders from Montreal and Quebec were pushing west and north-west from Michimilimackinac and Sault Ste. Marie into the territory left vacant by the withdrawal of French authority. These operators, acting independently, were collectively known as the Montreal traders.

In 1761, Alexander Henry formed a partnership with Étienne Campion, with their base at Michimilimackinac. Henry died on April 4, 1824 at Montreal.

Joseph, Thomas and Benjamin Frobisher, pioneer traders in the Lake Michigan area, combined with (Isaac) Todd and (James) McGill Company of Montreal, in 1769, to set up a post on Red River. They sent Thomas Curry to Fort Bourbon on Cedar Lake in 1770. Joseph Frobisher reached the Churchill River in 1771, and he built a post near the French Basquia (the Pas) in 1772, and Fort la Traite on the Churchill River in 1774.

Thomas Curry and François le Blanc, in 1772, formed a partnership on the Saskatchewan River that reached back to George

104

McBeath and Isaac Todd at Michimilimackinac and to Maurice
Blondell at Montreal and Judge Fowler Walker at Quebec.

James Finlay and John Gregory formed a partnership in
1773. Finlay retired in 1783, and his place was taken by Norman
McLeod. The firm became Gregory, McLeod and Company.

Alexander Henry, Benjamin Frobisher, Maurice Blondell
and James McGill, formed a four-way partnership in 1775. They
agreed to pool their trade goods and share the profits from the
Saskatchewan area in order to reduce competition. Working from
Michimilimackinac, the partnership was to run for one year.

Peter Pond made an agreement with George McBeath,
merchant of Montreal, in 1776, whereby the base was moved to
Grand Portage. By this saving in time, Pond could extend his
operation to the Athabaska country. The term North West Company
came into use at this time although there was no formal corporation.
Pond discovered Lake Athabaska in 1778, outfitted from the syndicate's post at Cumberland, and built his "Old Establishment, " 30
miles south of Lake Athabaska in September, 1778.

The North West Society was organized in 1779, on a six-
teen-share basis, held by nine different partnerships which included:
Montreal merchants Isaac Todd, James and John McGill, Simon
McTavish, Michimilimackinac trader George McBeath, Indian traders
Benjamin and Joseph Frobisher, John Ross and Peter Pond.

The Treaty of Paris on September 3, 1783, defined the
United States-Canadian boundary as running from the mouth of
Pigeon River on Lake Superior, along the Pigeon River-Rainy Lake-
Rainy River watershed to the northwest angle of Lake of the Woods,
then west along latitude 49° north to the point where it intersected
the Mississippi River. The last qualification was found to be an
impossibility.

The North West Company   1784-1821

In 1784, the syndicate re-organized, again on a sixteen-
share basis, and took the name North West Company, not a chartered corporation nor a limited liability company. Benjamin and Joseph
Frobisher, together with Simon McTavish controlled the most shares

105

and began to dominate the Company.   Peter Pond did not come in
until 1785.

Peter Pangman and John Ross, traders, formed a partner-
ship with Gregory, McLeod and Company of Montreal in 1785.
Gregory, McLeod and Company merged with the North West Company,
December 13, 1786 on a twenty-share basis, bringing in Alexander
MacKenzie, a partner in Gregory, McLeod and Company.

Benjamin Frobisher died April 14, 1787; Joseph Frobisher
and Simon McTavish combined in November, 1787, as McTavish,
Frobisher and Company to dominate the North West Company.
William McGillivray, McTavish's nephew, became a partner on
September 28, 1793.   Alexander Mackenzie became a partner on
November 4, 1793.

Fort Chipewyan on Great Slave Lake was built in 1789.   It
became the headquarters of the North West Company in the Athabaska district.   Roderick Mackenzie, cousin of Alexander Mackenzie, was its first chief.

The Jay Treaty dated November 19, 1794, was ratified on
June 24, 1795 to be effective on July 1, 1796.   It implemented the
1785 Treaty of Versailles.   It provided that the British must vacate
American territory.   This meant that Detroit, Michimilimackinac
and Grand Portage were legally denied to the Canadian traders.   It
did allow British and Canadian subjects to trade on either side of
the frontier and to travel on the waterways on either side of the
boundary or on the Mississippi River.

Joseph Frobisher retired on May 1, 1798.   William Mc-
Gillivray took his place; the company then became McTavish, Mc-
Gillivray and Company, and continued as the chief agent of the
North West Company.

The XY Company was organized in October, 1798.   A
partnership was formed by six wintering partners, backed by For-
sythe, Richardson and Company and Leith, Jamison and Company,
to compete against the North West Company.   Alexander Mackenzie
withdrew from McTavish, McGillivray and Company in November,
1799, to join this group, known variously as the New North West
Company, the XY Company, or Sir Alexander Mackenzie and Company.   (Mackenzie was knighted February 10, 1802).

The first canal was dug at Sault Ste. Marie by the North West Company in 1798, on the Canadian side of the rapids.

David Thompson established the location of the North West Company posts in relation to the United States boundary in 1797 to 1798.

Headquarters of the Company were moved from Grand Portage to Kaministikwia, where the first meeting was held June 9, 1803. The name of the post was changed to Fort William after William McGillivray. This name was first used at the meeting of June 5, 1808.

Simon McTavish died on July 6, 1804. The North West Company merged with the XY Company on November 5, 1804, on a 100-share basis.

Michimilimackinac Company was organized in 1804 by the North West Company to conduct trade in Michigan, Wisconsin and Minnesota. John J. Astor organized the American Fur Company, chartered in 1809 by the New York State legislature, to compete. The two merged on January 28, 1811, as the South West Company. This company dissolved after the beginning of the War of 1812.

For details of the merger with Hudson's Bay Company, see Joseph Berens, Jr., Governor of Hudson's Bay Company 1812-1822.

BRITISH COLUMBIA
Exploration and Claims   1774-1813

Juan Pérez, in the Santiago, sailing for Spain from Mexico, probably landed at Nootka Sound, Vancouver Island, August 7, 1774.

Bruno Hecata, in the Santiago, with Juan Pérez as co-pilot, landed at Point Grenville, latitude 47° 20' north, on the Washington coast, on July 14, 1775, claiming it for Spain. These were probably the first Europeans to land on the north west mainland.

Captain James Cook, in the Resolution, sailing for Great Britain, landed at Nootka Sound on May 29, 1778.

Captain John Meares, sailing in the Felice Adventurer for the East India Company, arrived at Nootka Sound on May 13, 1778. He built a house and then departed September, 1788.

Estevan José Martínez, in the Princesa, was sent by Revilla-Gigedo, Viceroy of Mexico, to establish Spanish claims. He arrived at Nootka on May 6, 1789.   Martinez seized Captain William Douglas and the British ship Iphigenia on May 14, 1789, and released them on May 26, 1789.   He took formal possession of Nootka port on June 24, 1789.   On July 4, 1789, he seized Captain James Colnett, in the British ship Argonaut, to prevent him from making a settlement for Great Britain.   He seized Captain Hudson and the British ship Princess Royal on July 14, 1789.   Colnett and Hudson were sent to San Blas, Mexico, where they were released and their ships were restored by the Viceroy in August, 1789. Martínez departed from Nootka on October 31, 1789.

Francisco Eliza took possession of Nootka port on April 10, 1790.   He erected a fort and commanded a garrison there from 1790 to 1792.

Alférez (second lieutenant) Manuel Quimper, in the Princesa Real, explored the Straits of San Juan de Fuca from May 31 to August 1, 1790.   He claimed the area for Spain at Neah Bay, Olympic Peninsula on August 1, 1790.

108

The Nootka Sound Convention, which was signed on October 28, 1790 at Madrid, restored the land and buildings at Nootka Sound seized by Martínez to the English. England secured, and Spain retained, rights of trade, navigation and settlement of the parts of the coast of North America not already occupied by Spain (north of Bodega Bay, California). Each nation was to have free access to the establishments of the other country in this area.

Captain Robert Gray, in the American ship Columbia, discovered the mouth of the Columbia River on May 11, 1792.

Don Juan Francisco de la Bodega y Cuadra was temporary Commander at Nootka from June to September, 1792.

Captain George Vancouver explored Puget Sound and took possession for Great Britain at Possession Sound on June 4, 1792. He named it New Georgia.

Lt. Jacinto Caamaño was temporary Commander at Nootka from September 7 to October 3, 1792.

Lt. Salvador Fidalgo was Commander at Nootka from September 7, 1792 to May, 1794.

Lt. William Broughton, in the Chatham, navigated the Columbia River upstream for 100 miles, from October 21, to November 10, 1792, and claimed the area for Great Britain at Point Vancouver.

Captain George Vancouver explored the coast from latitude 56° 30' north to 50° 30' north from May 26 to September 20, 1793. He named the area New Cornwall from latitude 56° 30' north to the Gardner Canal, and New Hanover from the Gardner Canal to New Georgia, and claimed the territory for Great Britain.

Alexander Mackenzie, exploring for the North West Company, started from Fort-of-the-Forks, at the Smokey River mouth of the Peace River, on May 9, 1793, and reached the Pacific Ocean at North Bentnick Arm on July 22, 1793. He returned to Fort Fork on August 24, 1793, and was the first to reach the Pacific by an overland route north of Mexico.

Alférez Ramon Saavedra was commander at Nootka from May, 1794 to March, 1795, when the provisions of the Madrid Convention were implemented at Nootka, on March 23, 1795, by General

José Manuel de Alva and Lt. Thomas Pierce, commissioners for Spain and Great Britain respectively. Both countries vacated the site at Nootka.

Organization of the Russian-American Company was confirmed by Tsar Paul I, in an Imperial Ukase, on August 11, 1799. This granted a monopoly of trade on the coast north of 55° north latitude for twenty years, and empowered the Company to extend southward into unoccupied territory. The first chief was Alexander Baranov, whose main post at Sitka was established on May 25, 1799. Baranov served until 1818.

Meriwether Lewis and William Clark, exploring for the United States, left St. Louis May 14, 1804, wintered at Fort Mandan on the Missouri River in North Dakota, and left there on April 7, 1805. They arrived at the mouth of Columbia River on November 14, 1805. Fort Clatsop, on Young's Bay, was occupied on December 12, 1805. Lewis and Clark started their return on March 23, and were back in St. Louis on September 23, 1806.

David Thompson, exploring for the North West Company, reached the headwaters of the Columbia River on June 30, 1807. He built Kootenay House at latitude 50° 32' 15" north, longitude 115° 51' 40" west. He left from Rocky Mountain House on October 11, 1810 and arrived at Tongue Point on July 15, 1811. He was the first to follow the Columbia River from source to sea. He found the Astorians at the mouth of the Columbia River.

Pacific Fur Company   1811-1813

The Pacific Fur Company was organized on June 23, 1810, by John J. Astor. It sent out two parties to the mouth of the Columbia River.

Duncan McDougall and Lt. Jonathan Thorn left New York City on September 8, 1810, in the Tonquin. They arrived at the mouth of the Columbia on March 22, 1811. Astoria was founded on April 12, 1811.

Wilson Price Hunt led an overland party from St. Louis on April 20, 1911 and when he arrived at Astoria on February 15, 1812, he took command. He left on August 26, 1813, to look for aid. Duncan McDougall sold out to John George McTavish of the North West Company on October 16, 1813, for $80,000.

The North West Company 1813-1821

John George McTavish took formal possession of Astoria for the North West Company on November 12, 1813.

John McDonald of Garth arrived on November 30, 1813, in the British frigate Raccoon under Captain Black, who took possession of the country for Great Britain on December 12, 1813. Astoria was renamed Fort George. Wilson Price Hunt returned on February 28, 1814 and left for good on April 3, 1814. Governor McDonald departed on April 4, 1814.

Donald McTavish was Governor in 1814. He arrived on April 7, 1814 to take over as Governor, but he was drowned on May 22, 1814, and was buried at Knappton, Washington.

James Keith was Acting Governor from the death of McTavish and was appointed Governor of the Coast on June 7, 1816 and served until 1821.

By the Treaty of Ghent on December 24, 1814, the area was restored to the United States.

The Columbia district was divided into two parts on June 7, 1816. James Keith was in overall charge at Fort George, and he also commanded the Coast district; Donald McKenzie was in charge of the inland district. He set up his headquarters at the junction of the Snake and Columbia Rivers on July 11, 1818 and called it Fort Nez Percé, which later became Fort Walla Walla, and is now Wallula.

Captain J. Biddle in the sloop of war Ontario, took formal possession of Ft. George for the United States on August 9, 1818.

J. B. Prevost, in the British frigate Blossom, and Captain Hickey received the surrender of Fort George on October 6, 1818 from James Keith. The North West Company was left in possession pending further arrangements, and Keith remained in charge.

The Convention of October 20, 1818, with Frederick Robinson and Henry Goulburn acting for Great Britain, while Richard Ruch and Albert Gallatin acted for the United States, set the United States-Great Britain boundary at latitude 49° north from Lake of the

Woods to the crest of the Rocky Mountains. It allowed joint occupation from the Rockies to the Pacific by citizens from both Great
Britain and the United States for 10 years. The agreement was
extended for an indefinite period on August 8, 1827, subject to
abrogation at any time by either party on twelve months' notice.

The Oregon-California boundary was fixed at latitude 42°
north on February 22, 1819, ending Spanish claims to the Columbia
area. John Q. Adams for the United States, and Luis de Oñis for
Spain were the negotiators.

Keith retired on March 21, 1821, when the holdings of the
North West Company passed to the Hudson's Bay Company.

Hudson's Bay Company   1821-1858

John Haldane was senior Chief Factor from August 13,
1821 until 1823. He was appointed by the Governor and Council of
the Northern Department of Rupert's Land and was to be stationed
at Fort George. John Dugald Cameron was appointed junior Chief
Factor.

The Imperial Ukase by Tsar Alexander I on September 4,
1821, forbade approach of all non-Russian commercial ships within
100 miles of the coast down to latitude 51° north. It also extended
the charter of the Russian-American Company another 20 years with
M. N. Mouravief named Governor to succeed Baranov.

John Dugald Cameron was appointed senior Chief Factor on
July 8, 1822. He was stationed at Fort George. Alexander Kennedy
was appointed junior Chief Factor. Cameron served until 1824.

Alexander Kennedy was senior Chief Factor from 1824 to
1825, and was stationed at Fort George. Dr. John McLoughlin was
appointed junior Chief Factor on July 10, 1824.

The Russian-American Treaty in April, 1824, fixed the
boundary at latitude 54° 40' north (Portland Canal) beyond which
neither nation was to found any establishment without permission of
the other. For ten years the vessels of either were to have free
access for trade and fishery to all interior waters of the other's territory. Middleton acted for the United States, and Nesselrode for
Russia.

The Anglo-Russian Treaty of February 28, 1825, relinquished

112

Russia's claims from latitude 54°40' north (Portland Canal) to longitude 141°west, then north to the Arctic Ocean. Russia retained what is now the State of Alaska. Subjects of both countries were to have free navigation and trade, for ten years, with the natives on any mainland shore not occupied by Europeans.

John McLoughlin arrived with Governor Simpson at Fort George, November 8, 1824 and was Chief Factor from 1825-1845.

The Fort Vancouver site was selected by Governor Simpson as the new headquarters of the Columbia district. The fort was christened on March 19, 1825 by Simpson, who departed on the same day, taking with him Alexander Kennedy, and leaving McLoughlin in control of the Columbia district.

Ft. Langley, at the head of sea navigation on the Fraser River, was settled on July 27, 1827 by Lt. AEmillius Simpson, captain of the Cadboro, and Chief Trader James McMillan, first chief (1827-1829). It was christened November 26, 1827.

On October 29, 1832, Nathaniel Wyeth and eleven American colonists arrived at Ft. Vancouver, traveling overland.

Jason Lee and nephew Daniel Lee, American Methodist missionaries, arrived at Ft. Vancouver, overland on September 15, 1834.

On March 22, 1838, McLoughlin departed for conferences in London. His duties were divided among three men: Chief Factor Peter Skene Ogden remained in charge of the New Caledonian section, with headquarters at Ft. James on Stuart Lake; Chief Trader James Douglas took command of the lower Columbia, the coasting trade and Ft. Vancouver; Chief Factor Samuel Black was given command of the Inland Posts on the Columbia. McLoughlin returned in October, 1839.

The Puget Sound Agricultural Company organized in February, 1839, to administer a Company colony around Ft. Nisqually. Nominally independent, it was actually under the control of, and owned by, the Hudson's Bay Company. It moved to Ft. Victoria in 1843, when the Company moved.

On July 1, 1839, Hudson's Bay Company obtained ten-year lease from the Russian-American Company, for trading in a strip of land ten leagues wide, extending north from latitude 54°40' north, and lying between British territory and the coast. The lease started on June 1, 1840, and was later continued to 1865, at which time, it was allowed to lapse. Alaska became United States property by purchase from Russia for $7,200,000 by Secretary of State William H. Seward, on March 30, 1867. The territory was transferred on October 18, 1867, at Sitka.

On March 16, 1843, Ft. Camosun started by Chief Trader James Douglas, with Charles Ross as its first chief. It was known locally as Ft. Albert from August to December 1843. It became Ft. Victoria after December 12, 1843, following a resolution of the Governor and Council of the Northern Department of Rupert's Land in June, 1843, and under instruction from Governor Simpson to McLoughlin on June 21, 1843.

On May 2, 1843, at Champoeg, Oregon, the American settlers voted to establish a provisional government, which was to continue in force until the United States Congress should establish territorial government.

The officials of a Provisional Government of Oregon were elected on the second Tuesday in May, 1844. The first legislature assembled at Oregon City on June 18, 1844.

In June, 1845, the Governor and Council of the Northern Department of Rupert's Land appointed a Board of Management to administer the Columbia District, which included New Caledonia. The Board consisted of McLoughlin, James Douglas and Peter Skene Ogden.

The Provisional Government of Oregon petitioned the United States Congress for territorial government on June 28, 1845.

George Abernethy was elected provisional governor in Oregon on the second Tuesday in November, 1845.

McLoughlin retired in November, 1845, and he was granted a three-year leave of absence preparatory to his official retirement on June 1, 1849. He moved to Oregon City in January, 1846 and became an American citizen on September 5, 1851. He died in Oregon City on September 3, 1857.

James Douglas became Senior Chief Factor and Chief of the

Board of Management of the Columbia District after McLoughlin's retirement in 1845. Chief Trader John Work was appointed to fill his former position and Chief Factor Peter Skene Ogden remained the third member of the group.

On June 15, 1846, the Oregon Boundary Treaty set the boundary at latitude 49°north from the crest of the Rocky Mountains to the Pacific Ocean. Great Britain got all of Vancouver Island. The Treaty was signed by President James K. Polk on June 18, 1846 and by Queen Victoria on July 17, 1846.

Hudson's Bay Company was granted a monopoly of trade on Vancouver Island, by Royal Charter on January 13, 1849. The Company received the grant in perpetuity, subject to revocation of the current "License for Exclusive Trade," which was to expire on May 30, 1859. The Company was to make a settlement and provide for representative government. It was given the mineral rights and was empowered to sell land.

Douglas took up official residence at Ft. Victoria in June, 1849. The Company used the Puget Sound Agricultural Company to provide for the non-fur trading functions under the above Royal Charter. Douglas was appointed agent on August 4, 1849.

Vancouver Island   1846-1866

Richard Blanshard was appointed Lt. Governor on July 16, 1849. His arrival on March 11, 1850, marked the establishment of a Crown Colony.

Blanshard appointed a Council of Vancouver Island on August 30, 1851, consisting of James Douglas, John Tod and James Cooper, and left on September 1, 1851.

James Douglas was Lt.-Governor from September, 1851 to 1864. He selected Roderick Finlayson to fill the vacancy on the Council. The Company's interests, as distinct from those of the colony, were still administered by the Board of Management, of which Douglas was still chief. He was also Agent for the Puget Sound Agricultural Company, which administered the colony.

In September, 1852, Douglas was given the additional office of Lt.-Governor of the Queen Charlotte Islands.

The first elected Assembly convened on August 12, 1856.
Dr. John S. Helmcken was its first Speaker.

Douglas severed his relations with the Hudson's Bay Company on November 19, 1858, and he was succeeded by Alexander G. Dallas (1858-1860) as Governor of the Board of Management of the Western Department for Hudson's Bay Company. Other members were John Work and Dugald McTavish.

Douglas died on August 2, 1877.

Arthur E. Kennedy took office as Lt.-Governor on March 25, 1864. He departed October 23, 1866. An Imperial Act, on August 6, 1866, united Vancouver Island with the mainland colony of British Columbia. The Proclamation was made November 19, 1866 at New Westminster.

New Caledonia 1805-1858

James McDougall built Ft. McLeod on McLeod Lake for the North West Company in the spring of 1805. This was the first post erected in this area.

Simon Fraser was in charge for the North West Company from 1805 to 1808. In 1805, he built Rocky Mountain House (now Hudson Hope) as a base for the New Caledonia area. This was the westernmost post east of the Rocky Mountains. He built Fort St. James on Stuart Lake in 1806 and Fort George (now Prince George), in 1807. Left there on May 28, 1808, and followed the Fraser River to the sea, arrived at its mouth on July 1, 1808, and returned to Fort George on August 6, 1808.

John Stuart was in charge for the North West Company from 1808 to 1821, and continued in charge after the merger with the Hudson's Bay Company on March 21, 1821. He was given the rank of Chief Factor by the Deed Poll of March 21, 1821. When he was appointed by the Governor and Council of the Northern Department of Rupert's Land on August 13, 1821 to take charge of the New Caledonia district, he set up headquarters at Fort St. James.

William Brown was Senior Chief Trader from July 10, 1824 to 1825. William Connolly was appointed Junior Chief Trader.

William Connolly was appointed Chief Factor on July 8, 1825, and served until 1831. New Caledonia was to be outfitted from Fort George on the Columbia River instead of from York Factory as heretofore.

On July 8, 1827, New Caledonia was designated as a section of the Columbia District. In theory, it was to be under Mc-Loughlin; in practice, McLoughlin left the management to the resident Chief Factor who was authorized to assign personnel to the various posts in his district.

Peter Warren Dease was appointed Chief Factor on July 7, 1830. He took command in April, 1831 and served until 1835.

Peter Skene Ogden, a Chief Factor since 1835, was appointed to the Board of Management of the Columbia District, which included New Caledonia, along with John McLoughlin and James Douglas, when that administrative body was created by the Governor and Council of the Northern Department of Rupert's Land in June, 1845.

James Douglas had final control of this territory by virtue of his position as Governor of the Board of Management for the Columbia (Western) Department of Rupert's Land. When gold was discovered in the Couteau region of the Fraser and Thompson valleys in 1856, and the gold rush began in March, 1858, the need for a more official government became apparent. Douglas, as Lt.-Governor of Vancouver Island, took authority although legally he had no jurisdiction. He issued orders in the name of "Her Majesty's Colonial Government" and as Chief Factor of the Hudson's Bay Company, starting from December 28, 1857.

British Columbia 1858-1871

The British Parliament passed an Act Providing for the Government of the Colony of British Columbia on August 2, 1858. The name was selected by Queen Victoria in a letter of July 24, 1858. The Colony was to include New Caledonia and the Queen Charlotte Islands. Vancouver Island was excluded, but provision was made for subsequent annexation.

Douglas was appointed Lt.-Governor on September 2, 1858, providing he severed relations with the Hudson's Bay Company, which

117

he did. He was inaugurated on November 19, 1858 at New Fort Langley, the capital. On the same date, he proclaimed the revocation of Hudson's Bay Company's License of Exclusive Trading Privileges and proclaimed the establishment of the Crown Colony of British Columbia. Douglas continued to reside in Victoria.

The capital moved to Queensborough, on February 14, 1859. Its name was changed to New Westminster by a Royal Proclamation on July 20, 1859. An agreement with the government on October 11, 1861, allowed the Company to keep up to 100 acres in the vicinity of each post and up to 500 acres around Kamloops and Ft. Langley.

The first legislative Council assembled on January 21, 1864.

Lt.-Governor, Frederick Seymour arrived on April 20, 1864, and died in office on June 10, 1869.

On August 6, 1866, an Act of Parliament united Vancouver Island with British Columbia. Seymour became first governor of the united colony.

First legislative Council of the United Colony of British Columbia met in New Westminster on January 24, 1867.

On April 3, 1867, Hudson's Bay Company relinquished all claims in Vancouver Island by Indenture of Surrender. The British government paid for all rights which the Company was able to make good.

The capital was changed from New Westminster to Victoria, on Vancouver Island, by a proclamation on May 25, 1868.

Anthony Musgrave was appointed Lt.-Governor in June, 1869. He began his term on August 23, 1869.

By Imperial Order-in-Council, May 16, 1871, effective July 20, 1871, British Columbia became a province of the Dominion of Canada, the 6th Province. Musgrave continued as Lt.-Governor until he departed July 25, 1871.

Lieutenant-Governors 1871-

Sir Joseph W. Trutch. Commissioned July 5, 1871.
Albert N. Richards. Commissioned June 27, 1876.
Clement F. Cornwall. Commissioned June 21, 1881.

Hugh Nelson. Commissioned February 8, 1887.

Edgar Dewdney. Commissioned November 1, 1892.

Thomas R. McInnes. Commissioned November 18, 1897.

Sir Henry G. Joly de Lothinière. Commissioned June 21, 1900.

James Dunsmuir. Commissioned May 11, 1906.

Thomas W. Paterson. Commissioned December 3, 1909.

Sir Frank S. Bernard. Commissioned December 5, 1914.

Col. Edward G. Prior. Commissioned December 9, 1919.

Walter C. Nichol. Commissioned December 24, 1920.

Robert R. Bruce. Commissioned January 21, 1926.

John W. F. Johnson. Commissioned July 18, 1931.

Eric W. Hamber. Commissioned April 29, 1936.

Lt.-Colonel William C. Woodward. Commissioned August 29, 1941.

Colonel Charles A. Banks. Commissioned October 1, 1946.

Colonel Clarence Wallace. Commissioned October 1, 1950.

Frank M. Ross. Commissioned October 3, 1955.

Maj.-General George R. Pearkes. Commissioned October 11, 1960.

Premiers 1871-

J. F. McCreight. Appointed November 13, 1871.

A. DeCosmos. Appointed December 23, 1872.

G. A. Walkem. Appointed February 11, 1874.

A. C. Elliot. Appointed February 1, 1876.

G. A. Walkem. Appointed June 25, 1878.

R. Beaver. Appointed June 13, 1882.

W. Smythe. Appointed January 29, 1883.

A. E. B. Davie. Appointed May 15, 1887.

J. Robson. Appointed August 2, 1889.

T. Davie. Appointed July 2, 1892.

J. H. Turner. Appointed March 4, 1895.

C. A. Semlin. Appointed August 12, 1898.

Joseph Martin. Appointed February 28, 1900.

James Dunsmuir. Appointed June 15, 1900.

E. G. Prior. Appointed November 21, 1902.

Richard McBride. Conservative. Appointed June 1, 1903.

William J. Bowser. Conservative. Appointed December 15, 1915.

Harlan C. Brewster. Liberal. Appointed November 23, 1916.

John Oliver. Liberal. Appointed March 6, 1918.

John D. Maclean. Liberal. Appointed August 20, 1927.

Simon F. Tolmie. Conservative. Appointed August 21, 1928.

T. D. Pattullo. Liberal. Appointed November 15, 1933.

John Hart. Coalition. Appointed December 9, 1941.

Byron Johnson. Coalition. Appointed January 18, 1947.

W. A. C. Bennett. Social Credit. Appointed August 1, 1952.

NORTH WEST TERRITORIES

Explorations

Eric Rauda - The Red, from Iceland, is claimed to have landed on Cumberland Peninsula, Baffin Island in 982.

Martin Frobisher made three voyages to Frobisher Bay, Baffin Island. The first was in 1576, for the Russia Company which was organized in 1555. The second and third voyages were for the Cathay Company in 1577 and 1578.

John Davis made three voyages to Davis Strait, between 1585 and 1587, for the North West Company. He described Hudson Strait in August, 1587, and he reached latitude 72°12' north, which he named Sanderson's Hope (near Upernivik, Greenland) in 1587.

William Baffin explored for the Governor and Company of the Merchants of London, Discoverers of the North West Passage, in 1615 to 1616, in Henry Hudson's ship, the Discovery. He named Sir Thomas Smith Sound, Sir Francis Jones Sound and Sir James Lancaster Sound, and reached latitude 76°, north in 1616.

Samuel Hearn explored for the Hudson's Bay Company in 1771. He reached the Arctic Ocean overland, via the Coppermine River, on July 18, 1771.

Captain James Cook, exploring for Great Britain, in 1770, in the Resolution, went through Bering Strait on August 11; to Icy Cape, Alaska on August 28, at latitude 71°17' north; to North Cape, Siberia, on September 1; and returned to Bering Strait on September 2, 1778.

Alexander Mackenzie, 1789, for the North West Company, started from Fort Chipewyan on Great Slave Lake, on June 3, 1789, and reached the outlet of the Mackenzie River on June 29. He reached the mouth of the Mackenzie River, on the Arctic Ocean on July 12 and returned to Fort Chipewyan on September 12, 1789. He was the first to follow the entire length of the Mackenzie River.

Edward Parry, exploring for Great Britain, in the Hecla,

121

with Lt. Liddon in the Griper, left England in May, 1819. They explored through Lancaster Sound, Barrow Strait and Melville Sound to longitude 110° west. They wintered at Winter Harbor, Melville Island and returned to England in 1820.

John Franklin, exploring for Great Britain, went overland from York Fort, via Fort Chipewyan and Fort Providence on Great Slave Lake. He built Fort Enterprise on Winter Lake and wintered there in 1820-1821. He explored from the mouth of Coppermine River eastward, and reached Point Turnagain, Kent Peninsula, on August 18, 1821.

Edward Parry explored the east coast of Melville Peninsula, and discovered Fury and Hecla Straits in 1822.

Lt. Ferdinand von Wrangel, exploring for Russia in 1823, proved conclusively that North American and Asiatic continents were separated. He completed the survey of the Siberian Coast, from Petropavlovsk to North Cape. As Baron Admiral von Wrangel he became the first Governor of Russian America (Alaska) and a director of the Russian-American Trading Company.

John Franklin, exploring for Great Britain started overland from Fort Norman on the Mackenzie River in 1825. Peter Warren Dease of the Hudson's Bay Company, and George Back, built Fort Franklin on Great Bear Lake as a base camp. Franklin and Dr. John Richardson separated at mouth of Mackenzie River on July 4, 1826. Franklin reached Return Reef (Beechey Point) longitude 150° west on August 16. Dr. Richardson reached the mouth of Coppermine River in August, 1826 and the parties met at Fort Franklin September 21, 1826.

Captain Frederick W. Beechey, exploring for Great Britain in the Blossom in 1826, examined the coast from Icy Cape to Point Franklin. Thomas Elson, master of the Blossom, reached Point Barrow by barge, on August 22, 1826.

John Ross explored for Great Britain in the Victory, from 1829 to 1833. His nephew, John Clark Ross, named Cape Franklin, Boothia Peninsula in 1830. On June 1, 1831, he was the first to describe the North Magnetic Pole (dip 89° 59' - latitude 70° 5' 17" north - longitude 96° 46'45" west). On May 31, 1831, he discovered

Bellot Strait, dividing Somerset Island from the mainland Boothia Peninsula, thus marking the northern extremity of the North American mainland.

George Back went overland for Great Britain in 1833 to 1834. He built Fort Reliance, on Great Slave Lake, as his base in 1833, then traced the Great Fish River - Back's River - to Montreal Island in 1834.

Thomas Simpson explored for the Hudson's Bay Company, in 1837 to 1839. Assisted by Peter Warren Dease, he set up his base camp at Fort Confidence. Simpson mapped the Arctic Coast between Return Reef and Point Barrow, reached Point Barrow on August 4, 1837. Victoria Island was named by Simpson on August 23, 1838. Simpson and Dease completed the mapping of the coast from Turnagain Point to Montreal Island by August 16, 1839, and were back at Fort Confidence by September 31, 1839. Simpson died on June 14, 1840.

Sir John Franklin explored for Great Britain in the Erebus and the Terror, in search of the North West Passage. He left London on May 19, 1845, and wintered at Beechey Island in Lancaster Sound. Franklin died June 11, 1847, and Captain F. R. M. Crozier, senior officer, abandoned the ships on April 22, 1848. The last record of this expedition was found at Victory Point and was dated April 25, 1848. Their fate was unknown until 1859.

On July 25, 1846, Dr. John Rae went overland, for the Hudson's Bay Company, from Repulse Bay, across Rae Isthmus to Committee Bay. He returned to Repulse Bay on August 10, 1846, and built Fort Hope as his base camp. Rae left there on April 5, 1847, and explored Committee Bay west. He reached Lord Mayor's Bay on April 18, 1847, and returned to Fort Hope on May 5; left there on May 13 to Cape Crozier, and returned to Fort Hope on June 9, 1847.

Captain Robert McClure explored for Great Britain in H. M. S. Investigator, via Bering Strait, from 1850 to 1853. He found a North West Passage through the Prince of Wales Strait, from Cape Lord John Russel, on October 27, 1850. The ship was frozen in the ice at Mercy Bay, Bank's Island. The crew abandoned the ship and were found on April 6, 1853 by Lt. Pim of the Belcher Expedition. The crew was taken home by Captain Henry Kellet of the same expedition in June, 1853.

Captain Richard Collinson explored for Great Britain in H. M. S. Enterprise, via Bering Strait from 1850 to 1859. He penetrated Dolphin and Union Strait, Coronation Gulf, Dease Strait, to Cambridge Bay, and Victoria Island. From there he sledged to Gateshead Island, proving another passage. He returned to England via Bering Strait and Cape Horn.

Commander E. A. Inglefield, in 1852, explored for Lady Jane Franklin, in the Isabel. He went through Smith Sound to Kane Basin, and named Ellesmere Island.

Leopold McClintock also explored for Lady Jane Franklin, in the steam yacht Fox, from 1857 to 1859. He completed tracing the coastline of Arctic North America, 120 miles on west coast of Boothia Peninsula in the winter of 1857 to 1858. It was he who discovered the last records and the fate of the Franklin Expedition at Victory Point on the north west shore of King William's Land on June, 1859.

Charles Francis Hall explored for the United States in the Polaris, in 1871. He penetrated Hall Basin and Robeson Channel to the Arctic Ocean at latitude 82° 11' north. He died of a stroke on the expedition.

Commander Albert Markham explored for Great Britain, in the Nares Expedition, in 1876, went through Robeson Channel, and sledged to latitude 83° 20' 26" north on May 11, 1876. Lt. Aldrich, of the same expedition, rounded Cape Columbia, Ellesmere Island, the northernmost point of land in Canada.

Otto Sverdrup exploring for Norway in the Fram, from 1898 to 1901, left Christiana, Norway, on June 24, 1898. He wintered near Hayes Sound in 1898-1899, and wintered at Havnefjord 1899-1900. He explored the Sverdrup Islands, and in the summer of 1900, went through Jones Sound and Cardigan Strait. The winter of 1900 to 1901 was spent at Gaasefjord, and he departed for home on August 8, 1901.

Roald Amundson led a Norwegian expedition in the Gjoa. He

left Christiana, Norway on June 16, 1903, and went through Lancaster Sound, Peel Sound, Franklin Strait, Sir James Ross Strait, Rae Strait. He spent two winters at Gjoehavn, and resumed the journey on August 13, 1905, through Simpson Strait, Queen Maude Gulf, Dease Strait, Coronation Gulf, Dolphin and Union Strait, Amundsen Gulf; and sighted Nelson Head, Banks Island on August 26, 1905. After wintering near Herschel Island, he resumed voyage in August, 1906, and reached Nome on August 31, 1906. He was the first to sail through a North West Passage.

Robert E. Peary, exploring for the United States, left Cape Columbia on February 28, 1909, and reached latitude 89° 57' (the North Pole) on April 6, 1909. He stayed there 30 hours and reached Cape Columbia on April 23, 1909.

Vilhjalmur Stefansson, a Norwegian, left the Karluk off Point Barrow, September, 1913. The Karluk was lost in the ice. Stefansson went overland across the Beaufort Sea to Banks Island and explored the area, living off the land. He started his return in August, 1917 and got back in 1918.

Old North West Territories 1869-1905

The Canadian territorial and administrative designation of North West Territories had its beginning in the passage on June 22, 1869, by the Parliament of Canada, of an Act for the Temporary Government of Rupert's Land and the North West Territories when United with Canada.

William McDougall was commissioned Lt.-Governor on September 28, 1869. For his subsequent actions, see the "Red River Rebellion, Assiniboia-Manitoba." He returned to Canada on December 18, 1869.

By Act of Parliament, on May 2, 1870, the name North West Territories was given to the portion of Rupert's Land and the north-western territory not included in Manitoba. The Act of June 22, 1869 was re-enacted temporarily for the new and limited North West Territories. It made the Lieutenant-Governor of Manitoba the Lieutenant-Governor of the North West Territories, as well.

Sir Adam G. Archibald was Lt.-Governor of Manitoba and

the North West Territories from 1870 to 1872. He was commissioned on May 20, 1870.

On June 23, 1870, by Imperial Order-in-Council, which
became effective of July 15, 1870, Rupert's Land and the old North
West territory were transferred to Canada, with the seat of Government at Fort Garry from 1870 to 1875.

Francis G. Johnson was commissioned Lt. -Governor of
Manitoba and the North West Territories on April 9, 1872.

Alexander Morris was commissioned Lt. -Governor of
Manitoba and the North West Territories on December 2, 1872.
He served in this capacity from 1872 to 1876, and he was Lt. -Gover-
nor of Manitoba until 1877.

An Act of Parliament on May 23, 1873, authorized the
establishment of the North West Mounted Police, which is treated
separately below.

An Act of Parliament on April 8, 1875, created the separate
political division of the North West Territories. The Act provided
for a resident Lieutenant-Governor and an appointed North West
Council which was given both legislative and executive powers.
Capital was to be at Battleford.

The last meeting of the legislative session of the Council at
Fort Garry was held November 23, 1875.

David Liard was Lt. -Governor of the North West Territories
from 1876 to 1881. He was commissioned on October 7, 1876.

In 1876, the District of Keewatin was created, covering the
northern part of Manitoba and western part of Ontario. This district
was taken from the jurisdiction of the North West Council, and placed
under the administration of the Lieutenant-Governor of Manitoba. Its
temporary seat of government in 1877, was at Fort Livingston on
Swan River. The first session convened on March 8, 1877. The
capital was moved to Battleford in 1878, and remained there until
1881.

On September 22, 1877, Treaty No. 7 was signed by Crow-
foot, chief of the Blackfoot tribe and Lt. -Governor Liard, at the
Blackfoot Crossing of the Bow River. This was the last important
treaty between the Indians and the Canadian government. It ceded to

126

Canada all Indian claims to land north of the international boundary, east of the Rocky Mountains and west of the Cypress Hills, and it ended Indian sovereignty in Canada.

An Imperial Order-in-Council dated July 31, 1880, and effective on July 31, 1880, annexed to Canada all British possessions in North America except Newfoundland. This applied in particular to the Arctic Islands, heretofore outside of any territorial jurisdiction.

Edgar Dewdney was Lt.-Governor from 1881 to 1888. He was inaugurated on December 3, 1881.

An Order-in-Council dated May 8, 1882, and effective on May 17, 1882, created the four provisional districts of Athabaska, Assiniboia, Alberta, and Saskatchewan with the capital at Regina.

The first session of the North West Council met at Regina on August 20, 1883.

Rebellion broke out on March 18, 1885. Louis Riel set up a provisional government at Batoche, Saskatchewan, March 19, 1885, with Pierre Parenteau as president and Gabriel Dumont as adjutant general. The North West Mounted Police under Superintendent L. N. F. Crozier was defeated by the Metis under Gabriel Dumont at Duck Lake on March 26, 1885. The Rebellion collapsed when government militia under General Sir Frederick D. Middleton captured Batoche on May 12, 1885 and Riel surrendered May 15, 1885. Big Bear and the Cree Indians surrendered to Major-General T. B. Strange near Fort Carlton on July 2, 1885. Riel was hanged on November 16, 1885, after a trial at Edmonton.

An Act of Parliament, dated May 14, 1886, provided representation for the territory in the Dominion parliament.

Joseph Royal was Lt.-Governor from 1888 to 1893. He was inaugurated on July 4, 1888.

The first elected legislative assembly, superceding the appointed North West Council, met in Regina on October 31, 1888.

Charles H. Mackintoch was Lt.-Governor from 1893 to 1898. He was inaugurated on November 1, 1893.

An Order-in-Council on October 2, 1895, enlarged the Athabaska District eastward and set up the provisional districts of

Yukon, Ungava, Mackenzie and Franklin.

On August 16, 1896, gold was discovered on Rabbit (renamed Bonanza) Creek, in the Klondike, by George Carmack, Skookum Jim and Tagish Charlie.

By Order-in-Council on August 16, 1897, the District of Yukon was created as a separate judicial district. The law was administered by a commission of six known as the Yukon Administration.

Complete responsible government, within the territorial status, was obtained on June 24, 1897, when an Executive Council, under Premier Sir Frederick W. G. Haultain (1897-1905), and having the confidence of the Legislative Assembly, assumed control of the territorial administration at Regina.

Malcolm C. Campbell was inaugurated as Lt.-Governor on June 7, 1898. He died in office at Regina on September 26, 1898.

Yukon was created a separate territory by Act of Parliament on June 13, 1898. The government was vested in a Commissioner and a legislative council partly elected and partly nominated by the Governor-General. The capital was at Dawson. For further details, see Yukon Territory.

Amédée E. Forget was inaugurated on October 13, 1898, as Lt.-Governor. He served until 1905 and then became Lt.-Governor of Saskatchewan from 1905 to 1910.

On July 25, 1905, the North West Territories Act set new boundaries which now excluded the Province of Manitoba, the forthcoming Provinces of Alberta and Saskatchewan, the Territory of Yukon and the District of Keewatin. It provided for a chief executive officer (the Commissioner) and an appointed Council. The Commissioner and Commission-in-Council received the same powers as those previously exercised by the Lieutenant-Governor, the Executive Council and the Legislative Assembly of the old North West Territories.

Alberta and Saskatchewan entered the Dominion of Canada as the 8th and 9th Provinces on September 1, 1905.

New North West Territories 1905-

Lt.-Colonel Frederick White was Commissioner from 1905 to 1919. He was appointed on August 24, 1905, and died in office in 1919.

The District of Ungava was absorbed in 1912 by extending the boundaries of Ontario and Quebec to Hudson's Bay. Ontario and Manitoba boundaries were extended to latitude 60° north, absorbing some of the District of Keewatin.

By Order-in-Council dated March 16, 1918, effective on January 1, 1920, the North West Territories were divided into the Districts of Keewatin, Mackenzie and Franklin, and their boundaries were set as they are today.

W. W. Cory was appointed Commissioner on June 27, 1919; and his term ended on February 17, 1931.

H. H. Rowatt was appointed Commissioner on March 31, 1931, and his term ended on April 30, 1934.

Maj.-General Sir James H. MacBrien, Commissioner of the Royal Canadian Mounted Police and Senior member of the Council. He was appointed Commissioner of the North West Territory on August 14, 1931.

Dr. Charles Camsell was appointed Commissioner on December 3, 1936, and his term ended on December 3, 1946.

Dr. H. L. Keenleyside was appointed Commissioner on January 14, 1947. His term ended on September 24, 1950.

H. A. Young was appointed Commissioner on November 14, 1950. His term ended on November 15, 1953.

An Act of Parliament in 1951, granted elected representation on the Territorial Council. The first partly-elected Territorial Council met at Yellowknife, Mackenzie District on December 10, 1951.

R. G. Robertson was appointed Commissioner on November 15, 1953. His term ended on July 12, 1963.

B. G. Sivertz was appointed Commissioner on July 12, 1963. His term ended on March 2, 1967.

January 18, 1967. Yellowknife was officially named the

Territorial Capital by the Honorable Arthur Laing, Minister of Indian Affairs and Northern Development, by authority of an Order-in-Council of the Governor-General.

Stuart M. Hodgson was appointed Commissioner on March 2, 1967.

ALBERTA

Lieutenant-Governors 1905-

George H. V. Bulyea. Commissioned August 24, 1905.

Robert G. Brett. Commissioned October 6, 1915.

William Egbert. Commissioned October 20, 1925.

William L. Walsh. Commissioned April 24, 1931.

Philip C. H. Primrose. Commissioned September 10, 1936.

J. C. Bowen. Commissioned March 20, 1937.

John J. Bowlen. Commissioned February 1, 1950.

J. Percy Page. Commissioned December 19, 1959.

J. W. Grant MacEwan. Commissioned January 6, 1966.

Premiers 1905-

Alex Rutherford. Liberal. Appointed September 2, 1905.

A. L. Sifton. Liberal. Appointed May 26, 1910.

Charles Stewart. Liberal. Appointed October 30, 1917.

Herbert Greenfield. United Farmers. Appointed August 13, 1921.

John E. Brownlee. United Farmers. Appointed November, 1925.

Richard G. Reid. United Farmers. Appointed July 10, 1934.

William Aberhart. Social Credit. Appointed September 3, 1935.

E. C. Manning. Social Credit. Appointed May 31, 1943.

SASKATCHEWAN
Lieutenant-Governors 1905-

Amédée E. Forget. Commissioned August 24, 1905.

George W. Brown. Commissioned October 5, 1910.

Sir Richard S. Lake. Commissioned October 6, 1915.

H. W. Newlands. Commissioned February 17, 1921.

Lt.-Colonel H. E. Munroe. Commissioned March 31, 1931.

A. P. McNab. Commissioned September 10, 1936.

Thomas Miller. Commissioned February 27, 1945.

Reginald J. M. Parker. Commissioned June 22, 1945.

J. W. Uhrich. Commissioned March 24, 1948.

W. J. Patterson. Commissioned July 4, 1951.

F. L. Bastedo. Commissioned September 1, 1958.

Robert L. Hanbridge. Commissioned March 1, 1963.

Premiers 1905-

Walter Scott. Liberal. Appointed September 12, 1905.

W. M. Martin. Liberal. Appointed October 20, 1916.

C. A. Dunning. Liberal. Appointed April 5, 1922.

J. G. Gardiner. Liberal. Appointed February 26, 1926.

J. T. M. Anderson. Conservative. Appointed September 9, 1929.

J. G. Gardiner. Liberal. Appointed July 19, 1934.

W. J. Patterson. Liberal. Appointed November 1, 1935.

T. C. Douglas. Cooperative Commonwealth. Appointed July 10, 1944.

W. S. Lloyd. Cooperative Commonwealth. Appointed November 7, 1961.

W. R. Thatcher. Liberal. Appointed May 22, 1964.

YUKON TERRITORY

Yukon was made a separate territory on June 13, 1898, by an Act of Parliament. The government was vested in a Commissioner and a legislative council partly elected and partly nominated by the Governor-General. The capital was at Dawson City.

James M. Walsh was Commissioner from 1897 to 1898. He was commissioned on August 17, 1897.

William Ogilvie was Commissioner from 1898 to 1901. He was commissioned on July 4, 1898.

On June 8, 1900, the White Pass and Yukon Railway was completed at Carcross, connecting Skagway, Alaska and Whitehorse.

James H. Ross was Commissioner from 1901 to 1903. He was commissioned March 11, 1901.

Frederick T. Congdon was Commissioner from 1903 to 1905. He was commissioned on March 4, 1903.

William W. McInnes was Commissioner from 1905 to 1907. He was commissioned on May 27, 1905.

Alexander Henderson was Commissioner from 1907 to 1912. He was commissioned on June 17, 1907.

George Black was Commissioner from 1912 to 1916. He was commissioned on February 1, 1912.

George N. Williams was Administrator from 1916 to 1918. He was appointed on October 13, 1916.

On March 28, 1918, the Offices of Commissioner and Administrator were abolished, and their powers were vested in the Gold Commissioner by Order-in-Council.

George P. Mackenzie was Gold Commissioner from 1918 to 1925. He was commissioned on April 1, 1918.

Percy Reid was Commissioner from 1925 to 1928. He was commissioned on April 1, 1925.

George Ian MacLean was Gold Commissioner from 1928 to 1932. He was commissioned September 10, 1928.

George A. Jeckell was appointed on June 30, 1932, with title of Comptroller. The title changed to Controller in December 1936. He served until 1947.

Alcan Highway, from Dawson Creek, British Columbia, to Fairbanks, Alaska, officially opened at Mile 1061, near Soldier Summit, on November 20, 1942.

John E. Gibben was appointed on September 18, 1947 as Controller. His title was changed to Commissioner on July 13, 1948, and he served until 1950.

Andrew H. Gibson was Commissioner from 1950 to 1951. He was commissioned on August 15, 1950.

Frederick Fraser was Commissioner from 1951 to 1952. He was commissioned on October 15, 1951.

Wilfred G. Brown was Commissioner from 1952 to 1955. He was commissioned on November 5, 1952.

On April 1, 1953, the capital was changed from Dawson City to Whitehorse.

Frederick H. Collins was Commissioner from 1955 to 1962. He was commissioned on June 8, 1955.

Gordon R. Cameron was Commissioner from 1962 to 1966. He was commissioned on May 1, 1962.

James Smith was named Commissioner on November 7, 1966.

ROYAL CANADIAN MOUNTED POLICE

An Act of Parliament on May 23, 1873, authorized the creation of the North West Mounted Police. Recruiting began in September, 1873. Lt.-Colonel Osborne Smith, Commanding Officer of the Winnipeg Military District, Lower Fort Garry, was acting Commissioner, and Superintendent W. D. Jarvis was in actual command pending the arrival of the first appointed Commissioner.

Major-General Sir George A. French was commissioned on October 16, 1873, and assumed his duties on December 17, 1873 at Lower Fort Garry. He served until 1876.

On June 19, 1874, the entire Force assembled at Dufferin, Manitoba, opposite Pembina, Minnesota. On July 8, 1874, they began a march to the forks of the Bow and Belly Rivers, in what is now Alberta.

October 9, 1874. Fort MacLeod begun, on Old Man River, near present Lethbridge, Alberta, under Assistant Commissioner Lt.-Col. J. F. MacLeod. Commissioner French returned east, wintered at Dufferin, and occupied barracks at Swan River, Manitoba, during the spring of 1875.

Lt.-Colonel James F. MacLeod was commissioned July 22, 1876, and served until 1880.

Beginning in 1876, the headquarters were at Fort MacLeod.

Beginning in 1879, the headquarters were at Fort Walsh, in the Cypress Hills of southwestern Saskatchewan.

Colonel Acheson G. Irvine was commissioned on November 1, 1880, and served until 1886.

The headquarters moved to Regina on December 6, 1882.

Colonel Lawrence W. Herchmer was commissioned on April 1, 1886, and served until 1900.

In July, 1895, Charles Constantine with a detachment, built Fort Constantine at junction of Forty-mile Creek and the Yukon River. He established Canadian law in the Yukon in September, 1897. When Constantine was succeeded by Superintendent S. B.

Steele, the headquarters moved to Dawson City.

Major-General A. Bowen Perry was Commissioned on August 1, 1900, and he served until 1922.

A post was established on Herschel Island in the Peaufort Sea in August, 1903.

On June 24, 1904, by permission of King Edward VII, it became the "Royal" North West Mounted Police.

A post was set up at Fullerton, on Hudson Bay near the Chesterfield Inlet, on September 23, 1904.

An Order-in-Council dated July, 1919, expanded its duties to include all of Canada west of Fort William.

An Act of Parliament, dated November, 1919, and implemented by an Order-in-Council on February 1, 1920, absorbed the Dominion Police into the Royal North West Mounted Police, moved it from Regina to Ottawa, and changed its name to the Royal Canadian Mounted Police.

Major-General Cortlandt Starnes was Acting Commissioner from April 1, 1922, and became Commissioner on April 1, 1923. He served until 1931.

The Royal Canadian Mounted Police absorbed the Provincial Police of Saskatchewan on June 1, 1928.

Major-General Sir James H. MacBrien was commissioned on August 1, 1931, and he died in office on March 5, 1938.

The Royal Canadian Mounted Police absorbed the Provincial Police of Manitoba and Nova Scotia on April 1, 1932.

They absorbed the Provincial Police of New Brunswick on April 30, 1932; the Provincial Police of Prince Edward Island on May 1, 1932.

On June 1, 1932, the Royal Canadian Mounted Police absorbed the Provincial Police of Alberta.

Colonel Stuart T. Wood was commissioned on March 6, 1938 and served until 1951.

The Newfoundland Rangers were absorbed on August 1, 1950, and the Provincial Police of British Columbia were absorbed on August 15, 1950.

Leonard H. Nicholson was commissioned on May 1, 1951

and he served until 1959.

Charles E. Rivett-Carnac was commissioned on April 1, 1959, serving until 1960.

Clifford W. Harvison was commissioned on April 1, 1960, and served to 1963.

George B. McClellan was commissioned on November 1, 1963.

M. F. A. Lindsay was commissioned August 15, 1967.

NEWFOUNDLAND

GREAT BRITAIN'S FIRST COLONY IN CANADA

Fishermen and Merchants versus Plantsrs 1497-1680

It is believed by some historians that it was Cape Bonavista that was sighted by John Cabot on June 24, 1497.

Devonshire fishermen from England may have begun to fish
around Newfoundland as early as 1498; the Portuguese in 1501; the
French in 1502; the Spanish and Basques not until 1545. From the
beginning until 1583, the island was free to all, with no country
claiming sovereignty.

The Devonshire fishermen and traders originated the practice of having the masters of the various ships in the fleet alternate
weekly as "admiral." On the basis of quarterdeck law, the admiral
settled all differences that arose among ship and shore personnel
in the particular harbor in which their shore establishment was
located.

By 1522, wintering crews were left behind to cut timber
for buildings and boats, when the fishing fleet returned to their
home ports at the end of the fishing season. The first settlements
were made between Cape St. Francis and Cape Race, and around
Conception Bay. From the beginning, ,St. John's was the headquarters of the fishing and trading activities on the island.

In 1578, assisted by Sir Walter Raleigh, Sir Humphrey
Gilbert obtained a charter from Queen Elizabeth, conveying to him
large tracts of land in the New World, including the island of Newfoundland. He was allowed six years to establish a viable claim.
He served as Governor from 1578 to 1583.

On August 5, 1583, in St. John's harbor, he claimed the
island for England, and gave title to the merchants for their shore
fishery sites. Sir Humphrey was lost at sea on November 9,
1583, while returning to England. His claim lapsed.

In the summer of 1585, during the war of Elizabeth against

Philip II, the English captured the Spanish fishing fleet off Newfoundland and took the ships and the men to England for disposal. After the defeat of the Spanish Armada on July 21-29, 1588, the Spanish came no more to the fishing grounds.

On May 2, 1610, James I granted a charter to the Company of Adventurers and Planters of the Cities of London and Bristol (Alderman John Guy's Company) to colonize from Cape St. Mary's to Cape Bonavista. In the summer of 1610, Guy brought settlers to Cuper's Cove, Conception Bay. He remained in Newfoundland until autumn of 1611, and made a second visit to his colony in 1612 to 1613. He then returned to England for good.

William Colston was Deputy Governor of Guy's Colony from 1613 to 1614. He was left in charge after Guy's departure.

Captain John Mason was Governor of Guy's Colony from 1615 to 1621. On June 14, 1615, Sir Richard Whitbourne convened a vice-admiralty court in Trinity Harbor to settle differences between the settlers and the fishermen; this was the first known court on the island.

Robert Hayman was Governor of Guy's Colony from 1621 to c. 1628.

In 1616, part of the claim of Guy's Colony was sold to Sir William Vaughn, who in 1621 sold part of his holdings to George Calvert. On April 7, 1623, King James I granted Calvert a charter in which his claim was designated as the Province of Avalon.

In September, 1621, Captain Edward Wynn, Calvert's deputy, brought 12 settlers, formed a colony at Ferryland. Calvert (Lord Baltimore from 1625) arrived with his family in 1628. He moved to Virginia in September, 1629 and died in 1632.

His son, Cecil, Lord Baltimore, sent Captain William Hill to Ferryland where he lived until evicted by Sir David Kirke.

On January 24, 1633, King Charles I, by Order from the Star Chamber, decreed that the captain of the first ship entering a harbor was to be admiral for the entire season, enforcing regulations and settling disputes on ship and shore.

On February 20, 1634, Charles I, by Order from the Star Chamber, granted a charter to the Western Merchants and Traders of Newfoundland. This charter gave preference to the fishermen and traders over the established settlers, and it prohibited settlements within six miles of the sea between Cape Race and Cape Bonavista.

On November 13, 1637, Charles I declared that all prior claims, including those of Guy's Company and Lord Baltimore, were to be vacated because the owners had abandoned the island. He granted to the Duke of Hamilton, Sir David Kirke, and others, the entire island, subject to the orders from the Star Chamber of February 20, 1634. Kirke had complete authority over all settlers on the island, but not over the fishermen, from 1637 to 1640.

Kirke came to Newfoundland in 1638, and moved into Baltimore's estate at Ferryland. He was recalled by the London partners on June 20, 1640, and was replaced as Governor by John Downing, Sr., London merchant.

The estate was confiscated by the Commonwealth of Cromwell in 1651; Sir David died June, 1653. The estate was restored to his brother, Sir James Kirke, by John Claypole, Cromwell's son-in-law in 1655.

In June, 1660, Lord Baltimore petitioned for the renewal of his patent. On June 17, 1660, Sir Oliver Bridgeman and Colonel Finch reported that the patent was still in force; a warrant was granted to Baltimore to take possession from the Kirke family. In 1661, Captains John Raynor and Pearce were at Ferryland to negotiate with the Kirke family. In 1662, Baltimore received a renewal of his patent.

The Kirke family was living at Ferryland in 1673 as ordinary citizens when Dutch raiders plundered the settlement.

On April 8, 1651, A Board of Commissioners, headed by John Littlebury, John Treworgie and Walter Sikes, was appointed by the Commonwealth to govern Newfoundland. They served until 1653.

John Treworgie was appointed sole governor by the Council of State of the Commonwealth on May 27, 1653. In June, 1653, the Council of State approved instructions to Treworgie regulating the government of the island, including the operation of the shore fisheries. Convoy captains were called on to assist him in enforcing the regulations.

With the Restoration of Charles II (May 29, 1660), interest in Newfoundland as a colony lapsed and the fishermen again gained the ascendancy. The island was left without government or defenses except those provided by the fishing admirals for three or six months of the year, depending on the season.

The charter of the Western Merchants and Traders was renewed on January 26, 1660. "All owners of ships trading to Newfoundland were forbidden to carry any persons not of the ship's company or such as are to plant or do intend to settle there."

Convoy Commodores 1661-1728

The Royal Navy began the practice of assigning a war ship to the Newfoundland Station in 1661. The war ship served as escort. It accompanied the fishing fleet from England to the fishing grounds, remained on the Newfoundland Station during the season, and escorted the fleet back to England at the close of the season. Gradually it became the custom to entrust certain judicial functions to the navy captain who commanded the escort ship; however, he had no authority in the ordinary affairs of the colony and fishery.

On June 6, 1665, as an incident of the Anglo-Dutch trade wars, Admiral Michael A. de Ruyter, Dutch commander, plundered St. John's, which was defended by the fishing admiral Christopher Martin.

Captain Robert Robinsen was Convoy Commodore in 1668.

Captain William Davis was Convoy Commodore in 1671.

Order-in-Council from Charles II on May 5, 1774, provided that the commander of the convoy was to advise the settlers "either to return home to England or to betake themselves to others of his Plantations; and to direct that letters be prepared unto the several Governors of the said Plantations that in case any of the said inhabitants of Newfoundland should arrive within their respective governments, that they should be received with favor. And that all convenient help and assistance toward their settlement be afforded unto them."

141

On January 27, 1675, a new charter was issued to the
Western Merchants and Traders. This confirmed the provisions
of the previous charters and added several new regulations: No
planter was to cut wood or inhabit within six miles of the shore;
no alien was to take bait or fish between Cape Race and Cape Bonavista; no master of a fishing vessel was to transport any seamen
or others to Newfoundland unless they belonged to the ship's company; masters were to give ₤100 bond to return all persons to
England except those employed in carrying fish to market; no fishermen was to remain in the country at the end of the voyage; admirals, rear-admirals and vice-admirals were authorized and required to preserve the peace in the harbors as well as on shore and
to see that the rules of the fishery were put in execution.

Captain Sir John Berry was Convoy Commodore in the
summer of 1675. The Western Merchants attempted to remove the
settlers by force; were restrained by the convoy commodore Sir
John Berry upon the petition of George Kirk of Ferryland, John
Pynn from Havre de Grace, John Downing from Que de Vide, and
Thomas Oxford from St. John's. John Downing appealed directly to
the Lords Commissioners for Trade and Plantations in London and
on March 28, 1677, a temporary restraining order was sent to the
Western Merchants in Newfoundland; it was confirmed on May 18,
1677.

Captain Edward Russell was Convoy Commodore in 1676.
Captain Sir William Poole was Convoy Commodore in 1677.
Captain Charles Talbot was Convoy Commodore in 1678.
Captain Wright was Convoy Commodore in 1679.
Captain Sir Robert Robinson was Convoy Commodore in 1680.
Captain Charles Hawkins was Convoy Commodore in 1691.
Captain Crawley was Convoy Commodore in 1692.

King William's War (1689-1697) in Newfoundland

Captain William Holman successfully defended Ferryland
against French raiders on August 31, 1694.

On November 30, 1696, the French under Pierre le Moyne,
Sieur d'Iberville and Jacques François de Brouillan, Governor of

Placentia, captured St. John's, which was defended by militia under Miners, a planter elected commander by the residents. The citizens were dispersed and the French went on to ravage other English settlements, returned to Placentia in March, 1697.

In 1697, Admiral Sir John Norris with Colonel Sir John Gibson, was sent to recapture Newfoundland. Norris, as commodore of the navy, was named Commander-in-Chief of the forces and also Governor of St. John's, a practice which was continued until 1703. Norris returned to England in the autumn of 1697.

The Treaty of Ryswick ended King William's War on September 20, 1697, and restored the status quo ante bellum.

Lt.-Colonel Handyside was Commander of the garrison from 1697 to 1698. New Fort William was constructed and, by order of King William on March 31, 1698, a permanent garrison was established. Garrison commanders were forbidden to interfere with the fishery, and only in cases of actual attack were they to exercise any authority over the settlers.

Captain Charles Norris was Convoy Commodore in 1698.

Lt. William Lilburn was Commander of the garrison, with 60 soldiers, from 1698 to 1699.

Captain John Leake was Convoy Commodore in 1699.

The Fishing Act of 1699 restricted the authority of the convoy commodores to enforcing the observance of the fishing rules and to acting as the final arbitrator for those who disagreed with the decisions of the fishing admirals. He was also to secure criminals and bring them to England for trial.

Captain Andrews was Commander of the garrison from 1699-1700.

Captain Sir Stafford Fairborne was Convoy Commodore in 1700.

Captain Graydon was Convoy Commodore in 1701.

Captain Sir John Leake was Convoy Commodore in 1702.

The War of the Spanish Succession began in Europe.

Captain Richards was Commander of the garrison up to 1703.

Lt. Thomas Lloyd was Commander of the garrison. He was

appointed on September 24, 1703 and was suspended by Captain Bridge, Commodore, September 7, 1704, on petition of the soldiers. He was named governor of St. John's, a practice which continued until 1709.

Lt. John Moody was Commander of the Garrison and Governor of St. John's from 1704 to 1705.

Lt. Moody successfully defended Fort William from the French under Daniel d'Auger, Sieur de Subercase, Governor of Placentia on January 25 - March 5, 1705. However, the town of St. John's was plundered, some citizens taken prisoner to Placentia, and other English settlements were laid waste.

Captain Thomas Lloyd was Commander of the Garrison and Governor of St. John's from 1705 to 1708.

On December 21-22, 1708, the French under Joseph de Saint Ovide de Brouillon, captured Fort William, and destroyed the fortifications. On January 8, 1709, Lloyd was sent as prisoner to Placentia, then to Quebec and on to France. On March 21, 1709, Saint Ovide returned to Placentia, taking prominent merchants along as prisoners. The citizens returned to St. John's on June 26, 1709.

Captain Joseph Taylour of the Royal Navy was Commander-in-Chief of English forces in Newfoundland.

On October 6, 1709, he appointed John Collins, Esquire, to be Governor and Commander of Fort William, the harbor of St. John's, and of all the coast between Ferryland and Carbonear Island.

Captain Joseph Crowe was the next Commander-in-Chief of H. M. ships, forts and garrison in Newfoundland. From August 23 to October 23, 1711, he held a voluntary assembly, consisting of merchant ship commanders and chief inhabitants, which acted as legislative, executive and judicial assembly.

Sir Nicholas Trevanion was the next Commander-in-Chief of H. M. ships and garrisons, and Governor-in-Chief of Newfoundland. Arrived September 17, 1712. He continued the idea of the voluntary meetings started by Captain Crowe.

Peace of Utrecht on April 11, 1713 gave Great Britain complete sovereignty over the entire island of Newfoundland including

Placentia; the islands of St. Pierre and Miquelon, and the mainland of Acadia (Nova Scotia). The French received Ile Saint Jean, Ile Royale, and all islands in the St. Lawrence River and the Gulf of St. Lawrence. In addition, the French received the right to fish off Newfoundland from Cape Bonavista to the northern point of the island and down the western side to Point Riche; in this fishing area they were permitted to live on land only during the fishing season and to erect buildings only for drying fish.

Placentia was put under the jurisdiction of the governor of Nova Scotia until 1729.

Captain Kempthorne was Convoy Commodore in 1715.

Captain Hagar was Convoy Commodore in 1716.

Captain Passenger was Convoy Commodore in 1717.

Captain Scott was Convoy Commodore in 1718.

Captain Ogle was Convoy Commodore in 1719.

Captain Percy was Convoy Commodore in 1720.

Captain Bowler was Convoy Commodore in 1722.

Lord Vere Beauclerk was Convoy Commodore in 1727.

Naval Governors 1729-1825

Starting in 1729, a naval officer attached to the convoy was given the title of Governor in order that he might create local magistrates to keep order during the several months of the year when there were neither fishing admirals nor king's ships on the coast. This established a system of civil government. In the same year, Placentia was put under the Governor of Newfoundland.

Captain Henry Osborne was Governor from 1729 to 1730.

Captain George Clinton was Governor in 1731.

Captain Falkinham was Governor in 1732.

Lord Muskberry was Governor from 1733 to 1736.

Captain Vanbrugh was Governor from 1737 to 1739.

George, Lord Graham was Governor in 1740.

The Honorable John Byng was Governor from 1741 to 1743.

Sir Charles Hardy was Governor from 1744 to 1746.

Captain Richard Edwards was Governor from 1746 to 1748.

Vice-Admiral Charles Watson was Governor in 1748. He

was appointed in March, 1748.

George Brydges Rodney, 1st Baron, was Commodore. Governor and Commander-in-Chief in Newfoundland in 1749.

Captain Francis William Drake was Governor from 1750 to 1752.

Captain Hugh Bonfoy was Governor from 1753 to 1754.

Captain Richard Doreill was Governor from 1755 to 1756.

Captain Richard Edwards (again) was Governor from 1757 to 1759.

Captain James Webb was Governor from 1760 to 1761. He died in office on May 14, 1761.

Captain Thomas Graves, 1st Baron Graves, was Governor from 1761 to 1763. St. John's surrendered to the French under Comte d'Haussonville, June 27, 1762. It was recovered by the British, under Lord Alexander Colville, on September 13 to 18, 1762. By the Treaty of Paris on February 10, 1763, Newfoundland was retained by Great Britain but the islands of St. Pierre and Miquelon were given to the French.

By Royal Proclamation on October 7, 1763, Labrador was annexed to Newfoundland.

Sir Hugh Palliser was Governor from 1764 to 1769.

Commodore John Byron was Governor from 1769 to 1772.

Commodore Molyneux, Baron Shuldham was Governor from 1772 to 1775. The Quebec Act, June 22, 1774, put Labrador under the control of Quebec.

Commodore Robert Duff was Governor from 1775 to 1776.

Rear-Admiral John Montague was Governor from 1776 to 1779. He arrived on May 7, 1776.

Rear-Admiral Richard Edwards was Governor for the third time from 1779 to 1782.

Vice-Admiral John Campbell was Governor from 1782 to 1786.

The Crown ruled that neither the Governor nor the officers of his ships could judge civil cases.

The Treaty of Paris, on September 3, 1783, permitted the French to fish from Cape John to Cape Ray.

Rear-Admiral John Elliot was Governor from 1786 to 1789.

The Court of Common Pleas was established for the colony in 1789.

Admiral Mark Milbank was Governor from 1790 to 1792.

Sir Richard King, 1st Baronet, was Governor from 1792 to 1793.

The Supreme Court of Judicature convened on September 7, 1792, presided over by Chief Justice Reeves.

The islands of St. Pierre and Miquelon were captured by the British in 1793.

Vice-Admiral Sir James Wallace was Governor from 1794 to 1797.

France declared war on Great Britain in 1794.

Vice-Admiral Sir William Waldegrave was Governor from 1797 to 1800.

Admiral Sir Charles M. Pole was Governor from 1800 to 1801.

Admiral James, Baron Gambier was Governor from 1802 to 1804.

St. Pierre and Miquelon were returned to the French by the Treaty of Amiens on March 27, 1802.

Sir Erasmus Gower was Governor from 1804 to 1807.

Admiral John Holloway was Governor from 1807 to 1809. He arrived on July 26, 1807.

The authority of fishing admirals was ended by statute.

Labrador and Anticosti were re-annexed to Newfoundland.

Vice-Admiral Sir John Duckworth, 1st Baronet, was Governor from 1810 to 1813.

Sir Richard Godwin Keats was Governor from 1813 to 1816.

Vice-Admiral Francis Pickmore was Governor from 1816 to 1818. He died in office February 24, 1818.

Captain Bowker was Administrator from February 24, 1818 to July, 1818.

Sir Charles Hamilton was Governor from 1818 to 1824. He arrived July, 1818.

An Act of Parliament in 1824 recognized Newfoundland as a Crown Colony, but did not grant an Assembly.

Resident Governors 1825-1855

Sir Thomas Cochrane was Governor from 1825 to 1834. He was the first resident Governor.

The coast of Labrador inside of Belle Isle Strait was annexed to Lower Canada (Quebec) in 1825.

The Supreme Court of Newfoundland was constituted by Royal Charter, and it convened January 2, 1826, under Chief Justice Tucker.

Representative government was granted to the colony through an elected general assembly in 1832.

The first elected general assembly opened on January 1, 1833 at St. John's; John B. Garland, was the first speaker.

Captain Sir Henry Prescott was Governor from 1834 to 1841. Legislature dissolved, constitution suspended, April 26, 1841.

Major-General Sir John Harvey was Governor from 1841 to 1846. He arrived on September 16, 1841, and was re-assigned to Nova Scotia in 1846.

On August 12, 1842, the constitution was revised; the appointed legislative council was merged with the elected assembly, providing a unicameral legislature.

The new legislature convened at St. John's on January 17, 1843.

Colonel Law was Administrator until April 23, 1847.

Sir John Gaspard LeMarchant was Governor from 1846 to 1852. He arrived on April 23, 1847, and departed on July 28, 1852 to become Governor of Nova Scotia.

The bicameral Legislature was restored in 1848, and convened on December 14, 1848.

Ker Baille Hamilton was Governor from December, 1852 to 1855.

Responsible Government 1855-1933

Sir Charles H. Darling was Governor from 1855 to May, 1857.

An executive council (cabinet) was created, distinct from the legislative council (upper house); having full ministerial responsibility and the confidence of the Assembly (lower house).

Philip F. Little, leader of the Liberal Party, who had the majority in the Assembly which convened May 7, 1855, was appointed as first Prime Minister. This legislature was the beginning of responsible government in Newfoundland.

Honorable L. O'Brien. Administrator. President of the Council

Sir Alexander Bannerman was Governor from 1857 to 1863. He was formerly Lieutenant-Governor of Prince Edward Island.

John Kent's ministry, Liberal was appointed in 1858.

Sir Hugh Hoyles' ministry, Conservative, was appointed in 1861.

Honorable L. O'Brien. Administrator. He was President of the Council.

Sir Anthony Musgrave took office as Governor in April, 1864. He left in June, 1869 to become Lieutenant-Governor of British Columbia.

Sir Frederick Carter's ministry, Liberal, was appointed in 1865.

Sir Stephen J. Hill was appointed Governor in July, 1869 and served until 1875.

Charles F. Bennett's ministry, Conservative, was appointed in 1869.

Sir Frederick Carter, Liberal, was re-appointed Minister in 1874.

Sir John H. Glover was Governor from 1875 to 1881.

Sir William V. Whiteway's ministry, Liberal, was appointed in 1878.

Sir Henry B. F. Maxse was Governor from 1881 to 1883. He died in office on September 10, 1883.

Sir Frederick Carter. Administrator. He was now Chief Justice of the Supreme Court.

Sir John H. Glover, was Governor again from 1883 to 1885. He arrived in July, 1883, and died in office while in England on

September 30, 1885.

Sir Robert Thorburn's ministry, Conservative, was appointed in 1885.

Sir Frederick Carter was Administrator. Chief Justice of the Supreme Court.

Sir G. William Des Voeux was Governor in 1886.

Sir Frederick Carter was Administrator. Chief Justice of the Supreme Court.

Sir Henry A. Blake was Governor from January 1887 to 1889. He arrived in January, 1887.

Sir William V. Whiteway, Liberal, was re-appointed Minister in 1889.

Sir Frederick Carter was Administrator. Chief Justice of the Supreme Court.

Sir John Terence O'Brien was Governor from 1889 to 1896.

Augustus F. Goodridge's ministry, Conservative, was appointed in April, 1894.

Daniel J. Green's ministry, Liberal, was appointed on December 13, 1894.

Sir William V. Whiteway became Minister for the third time, Liberal, appointed in February, 1895.

Sir Herbert H. Murray was Governor from 1895 to 1898.

Sir James S. Winter's ministry, Conservative, was appointed October, 1897.

Sir Henry E. McCallum was Governor from 1898 to 1901.

Sir Robert Bond's ministry, Liberal, was appointed 1900.

Sir Cavendish Boyle was Governor from 1901 to 1904.

Sir William MacGregor was Governor from 1904 to 1909.

Sir Edward P. Morris' ministry, People's Party, was appointed 1909.

Sir Ralph C. Williams was Governor from 1909 to 1913.

Sir Walter E. Davidson was Governor from 1913 to 1917.

Sir C. Alexander Hamilton was Governor from 1917 to 1922.

The Morris ministry resigned in January, 1918, and Sir John C. Crosbie became acting Prime Minister.

Sir Edward P. Morris, People's Party, was re-appointed Minister in 1918.

Sir William F. Lloyd's ministry, Liberal, was appointed in 1918.

Sir Michael Cashin's ministry, Conservative, was appointed May, 1919.

Sir Richard A. Squires' ministry, Liberal, was appointed 1919.

Sir William L. Allardyce was Governor from 1922 to 1929.

William R. Warren's ministry, was appointed July, 1923.

Albert E. Hickman's ministry, Liberal, was appointed May, 1924.

Walter S. Monroe's ministry, Conservative, was appointed 1924.

On March 21, 1927, as a result of deliberations of the Judicial Committee of the British Privy Council, the Labrador coast was annexed to Newfoundland.

Sir John Middleton was Governor from August, 1928 to 1932.

Frederick C. Aldendice's ministry, Conservative, was appointed 1928.

Sir Richard A. Squires, Liberal was re-appointed Minister in November, 1928.

Frederick C. Aldendice, Conservative, was re-appointed Minister in 1932.

Crown Colony of Newfoundland 1933-1949

Sir David M. Anderson was Governor from 1933 to 1934. The Dominion status was lost and the constitution was suspended on December 2, 1933. Newfoundland reverted to the status of a Crown Colony, Governor Anderson presided over the commission that took the place of the legislature. The commission was appointed in London. It consisted of three Newfoundlanders and three non-Newfoundlanders.

The Aldendice ministry ended February 15, 1934.

Vice-Admiral Sir Humphrey T. Walwyn was Governor-General from 1934 to 1940. He was inaugurated on February 16, 1934.

Earl of Athlone was Governor-General from 1940 to 1946. He was inaugurated on June 21, 1940.

Sir Gordon Macdonald, 1st Baron, was Governor-General from 1946 to 1949. He was the last Governor-General before Newfoundland entered the Dominion of Canada on March 31, 1949, as the 10th Province, under the provisions of the British North American Act of 1949.

Province of Newfoundland   1949-

Lieutenant-Governors

Sir Albert J. Walsh. Commissioned April 1, 1949.
Lt.-Col. Sir Leonard Outerbridge. Commissioned September 5, 1949.
Campbell MacPherson. Commissioned December 16, 1957.
Fabian O'Dea. Commissioned March 1, 1963.

Premiers

Joseph R. Smallwood. Liberal. Appointed April 1, 1949.

Placentia 1662-1729

Placentia was founded about 1640 by the French, but no French wintered there until 1662.

Sieur de Keréon, Breton, received a commission as Governor of Newfoundland from Louis XIV, in 1655. He was opposed by the fishermen of St. Malo, and nothing came of it.

Captain Nicolas Gargot, in 1658, received the title of Count of Newfoundland from Louis XIV, and a concession of land. He fortified Placentia in 1662 and commanded the area from Cape Race to Cape Bonavista. French fishing admirals were subject to orders from the Governor of Placentia. Settlement was encouraged.

Thalour du Perron commanded a small party at Placentia, in 1662. He murdered another French commander, Sieur Billot. Placentia claimed control from Cape Ray to Cape Race.

Bellot de la Fontaine was Commander from 1664.

Sieur de Palme was Commander from December 31, 1667 to 1670.

The term of Sieur de la Poëpe as Governor extended from February 20, 1670 to January 13, 1685.

Placentia fort was reported to be in ruins in 1681.

Antoine Parat was Governor from June 2, 1685 to September 28, 1690.

In 1685, the defenses were repaired.

Jacques François de Brouillan was commissioned Governor on June 1, 1690, was in office from 1691 to April 1, 1702.

In 1692, a garrison under de Montorgueil was installed. It defended against the British under Commodore Williams in September 1692 and in 1693.

French under d'Iberville and Governor Brouillan captured St. John's on November 30, 1692. The Treaty of Ryswick on September 20, 1697, restored the status quo ante bellum.

Brouillan was appointed Governor of Acadie in 1701.

Daniel d'Auger, Sieur de Subercase was commissioned as Governor on April 1, 1702. He was in office from June 9, 1703 to September, 1706, and was appointed Governor of Acadie on April 10, 1706.

Philippe de Costabelle was commissioned as Governor on April 10, 1706, and was in office from September, 1706 to 1714.

Under the Peace of Utrecht, on April 11, 1713, France recognized British sovereignty and relinquished territorial rights to Acadie and Newfoundland, but kept Ile Royale and Ile Saint Jean. The islands of St. Pierre and Miquelon, heretofore regarded as French, went to Great Britain.

Governor Costabelle delivered Placentia to the English under Captain John Moody, June 1, 1714 (O. S.), and moved to Ile Royale where he was appointed Governor.

Captain John Moody was Lieutenant-Governor of Placentia from 1714 to 1719. Placentia was put under the Governor of Nova Scotia.

Colonel Richard Philipps was Governor of Nova Scotia from 1717 to 1749. His commission was dated July 9, 1719. It named him Governor of Placentia and Captain-General and Commander-in-Chief of Nova Scotia.

Colonel Gledhill was appointed Lieutenant-Governor of Placentia, 1719.

In 1729, Placentia was put under the governorship of Newfoundland.

Bibliography

Audet, Francis J. Canadian Historical Dates and Events. Ottawa, George Beauregard, 1917.

Bancroft, H. H. "Alaska, 1730-1885" (In History of the Pacific States, Vol. 28). San Francisco, A. L. Bancroft, 1886.

Beck, J. Murray The Government of Nova Scotia. Toronto, University of Toronto Press, 1957.

Brebner, J. B. New England Outpost: Acadia before the Conquest of Canada. Hamden, Connecticut, Archon Books, 1965.

Burpee, Lawrence J. The Search for the Western Sea. Toronto, Musson Books, 1908.

"Canada and Newfoundland" (In Cambridge History of the British Empire, Vol. 6). New York, Macmillan, 1930.

Crouse, Nellis M. LaVerendrye, Fur Trader and Explorer. Ithaca, New York, Cornell University Press, 1956.

Encyclopedia Canadiana. 10 Volumes. Ottawa, The Grolier Society of Canada, Ltd., 1960.

Fetherstonhaugh, R. C. The Royal Canadian Mounted Police. New York, Carrick & Evans, 1938.

Harvey, D. C. The French Regime in Prince Edward Island. New Haven, Yale University Press, 1926.

History of Modern Louisburg 1758-1958. Louisbourg Branch of the Womens Institute of Nova Scotia.

Lanctot, Gustave A History of Canada. Cambridge, Massachusetts, Harvard University Press, 1963.

MacKinnon, Frank The Government of Prince Edward Island. Toronto, University of Toronto Press, 1951.

MacNutt, W. S. New Brunswick, A History: 1784-1867. Toronto, MacMillan of Canada, 1963.

Mirsky, Jeanette To the Arctic. New York, Alfred A. Knopf, 1948.

Murdoch, Beamish A History of Nova Scotia. 3 vols. Halifax, Nova Scotia, James Barnes, Printer & Publisher, 1865.

Prowse, D. W. A History of Newfoundland. London and New York, MacMillan, 1895.

Rich, E. E. The Hudson's Bay Company. London, Hudson's Bay Record Society, Vol. 21, 1958, Vol. 22, 1959.

Sage, Walter N. Sir James Douglas and British Columbia. Toronto, University of Toronto Press, 1930.

Shortt, Adam & Doughty, Arthur G. Canada and Its Provinces, Volume 23. Toronto, Glasgow, Brook & Co. 1917.

Scholefield, E.O.S., and Howay, F.W. British Columbia, 2 Vols. Vancouver, Winnipeg, Montreal, Chicago, S.J.Clark Publishing Co. No date.

Urquhart, M.C., Editor Historical Statistics of Canada. Toronto, Cambridge University Press, 1965.

Voorhis, Ernest Historic Forts and Trading Posts of the French Regime and of the English Fur Trading Companies. Department of the Interior, Ottawa, 1930.

Index

A

B

158

161

164

MacTavish, William 94, 98, 99
Mainwaring, William 80, 81
Maisonneuve, Sieur de 19
Maitland, Peregrine 30, 33, 53
Malecite Indians x
Manitoba 37, 125, 128
  Assiniboia Colony 95-98
  Lieutenant-Governors 100-101
  Premiers 101
  Provincial Police 136
  Red River Rebellion 98-100
Manning, E. C. 131
Marchand, F.-Gabriel 41
Marcy, William L. 83
Markham, Albert 124
Marquette, Father Jacques 22
Marsh, John 87
Marson, Sieur de 47
Marten, Humphrey 91, 92
Martin, Christopher 141
Martin, Joseph 119
Martin, W. M. 132
Martínez, Estevan José 108
Mary I xiii
Mary II xiii
Mascarene, Paul 49
Mason, John 139
Massey, Vincent 40
Masson, L. F. R. 40
Mathers, Frederick F. 55
Matheson, A. W. 71
Mathews, D. 76
Mathieson, John A. 70
Matonabbee 91
Matthews, Albert 42
Maugenest, Germain 80
Maxse, Henry B. F. 149
Maxwell, Murray 67
McBeath, George 104, 105
McBride, Richard 119
McCallum, Henry E. 150
McClelan, A. R. 60
McClellan, George B. 137
McClintock, Leopold 124
McClure, Major-General 33
McClure, Robert 123
McCreight, J. F. 119
McCurcy, J. A. D. 55
McDiarmid, John S. 101
McDonald, John, of Garth 111
McDouall, Robert 33
McDougal, William 98, 99

McDougall, Duncan 110
McDougall, James 116
McDougall, William 84, 85, 125
McGill, James 104, 105
McGill, John 105
McGillivray, Simon 81-83
McGillivray, William 82, 83, 96, 106
McGregor, J. D. 101
McGregor, James D. 55
McInnes, Thomas R. 119
McInnes, William W. 133
McIntyre, P. A. 70
McKenzie, Donald 97
McLean, Hugh H. 60
McLeish, Thomas 90
McLelan, A. W. 55
McLeod, N. 70
McLeod, Norman 105
McLoughlin, John 112-114, 117
McMillan, Daniel H. 100
McMillan, James 113
McNab, A. P. 132
McNair, J. B. 61
McNair, John B. 60
McTavish, Donald 111
McTavish, Dugald 116
McTavish, Frobisher & Co. 106
McTavish, John George 110, 111
McTavish, McGillivray & Co. 106
McTavish, Simon 105-107
McWilliams, Roland F. 101
Meares, John 108
Meighen, Arthur 38
Melville Island 122
Melville Peninsula 122
Melville Sound 122
Menneval, Chevalier de 48
Menneville, Marquis de 24
Mercier, Honore 41
Mercy Bay 123
Merry, John 80
Merry, Robert 80
Metcalfe, Charles, Lord 35
Métis 95, 96, 127
Meulles, Jacques de 22
Mezy, Jacques de 73
Mezy, Sebastien de 73
Mezy, Sieur de 21
Michener, Roland 40
Michimilimackinac 104-106

172

von Wrangel, Ferdinand 122

W

Wakashan Indians ix
Waldegrave, William 147
Walker, G.A. 119
Walker, Fowler 105
Walker, Hovenden 73
Walker, Richard 47
Wallace, Clarence 119
Wallace, James 147
Wallace, Michel 53
Wallula, Washington 111
Walsh, Albert J. 152
Walsh, James W. 133
Walsh, Thomas 89
Walsh, William L. 131
Walwyn, Humphrey T. 151
Warburton, A.B. 70
War of 1812 32-33
War of the Austrian Succession
  50, 64, 74 -see also
  King George's War
War of the Spanish Succession
  48 -see also Queen Anne's
  War
Warren, Admiral 64
Warren, Peter 74
Warren, William R. 151
Watson, Charles 145
Watteville Regiment 96
Webb, Major 98
Webb, James 146
Webster-Ashburton Treaty 58
Wedderburn's Retrenching System
  81, 92
Wegg, Samuel 80
Weir, Walter 101
Welland Canal 33
Wentworth, John 53
Wetmore, A.R. 60
Whitbourne, Richard 139
White, Frederick 129
White, Thomas 91
Whitehorse 133, 134
White Pass & Yukon Railway
  133
Whiteway, William V. 149, 150
Whitmore, Edward 75
Whitney, J.P. 42
William III xiii
William IV xiii

Williams, Commodore 153
Williams, George N. 133
Williams, Ralph C. 150
Williams, William 93, 94
Williams, William F. 55
Willingdon, Viscount 40
Willis, Errick F. 101
Wilmot, Lemeul A. 60
Wilmot, Montague 51
Wilmot, Robert D. 60
Wilson, John 29
Winnipeg (city) 97
Winnipeg District, Rupert's Land
  93
Winslow, Edward 57
Winter Harbor 122
Winter, James S. 150
Winter Lake 122
Wolfe, James 25, 75
Wolseley, Garnet 100
Wood, Josiah 60
Wood, Stuart T. 136
Woodward, William C. 119
Work, John 115, 116
Wright, Captain 142
Wright, George 67, 68
Wyeth, Nathaniel 113
Wynn, Edward 139

X-Y-Z

XY Company 106, 107
Yellowknife 129, 130
Yellowknife Indians ix
York, Duke of 79
York Fort 82, 87-90, 92-94, 96
York (Toronto) 32-34
Young, Aretas W. 67
Young, Charles 68
Young, H.A. 129
Young, William 54
Yukon 128, 135
  Territory, Commissioners
  133-134